THE CONCERNS
OF
RELIGION

The Concerns
of
Religion

ARTHUR C. WICKENDEN

HARPER & BROTHERS PUBLISHERS
NEW YORK

TO

ETHEL R. WICKENDEN

Contents

Contents

Foreword

THIS work has been published in two previous editions under the title *Youth Looks at Religion*. Although the book was designed to meet the needs of thinking young people, it has been found helpful by many general readers, and in bringing out a new revised edition it seems well to give it a new name which would better connote the nature of its contents. It is the product of years of dealing with the religious problems of young people in the classroom and in conferences, and these experiences made me aware of the need for a book which would serve young people and their leaders as a suitable resource in this field. The book required was a simple discussion of the questions which arise naturally in the thinking of young people and comprehensive in the range of subjects discussed. The present work seeks to fulfill those specifications. The principal change from the earlier revised edition is a rewriting of Chapter XIII, "Religion and Social Change," to bring the discussion up to date, and to deal with the issues more adequately. A significant addition has been made to Chapter V which discusses the Bible, and lesser changes and additions have been made to several other chapters.

A generation of youth which is religiously illiterate, and many of their elders as well, are wistful for a faith by which to live in a tragic age, and are ready to consider seriously the claims and resources of religion. The object of this work is not to tell its readers what they must think or believe about religious questions, but to help them see where the Christian world in particular is in its thinking and faith. There are various approaches made by different groups of equally earnest people to the insistent questions of life and religion, and an effort is made to review and compare ideas that are typical of large groups within Christendom. With the help of such a survey it is hoped that inquiring readers will be furnished with an elementary background that will enable them to launch out on a further course of thinking for themselves, and perhaps find here some materials that will serve them in constructing their own houses of faith.

While the questions raised are largely those which are asked by young people when they start to think seriously about religious problems, in the discussion of them an endeavor is made to go beyond the initial questions and to suggest some problems to the readers which will tend to push out the horizons of their thought and cause them to face some of the great challenges of our time.

I am happy to renew an acknowledgment made in the first edition of the book of the generous help received from two former colleagues in the ministry of religion to the students of Miami University. Dr. C. E. Conover, now professor of philosophy at Lindenwald College, and the Reverend Eliot Porter, Ph.D., read early drafts of the manuscript and made valuable suggestions for its development. Other sources of help are too numerous to mention, but the appended bibliography will throw some light on these.

A WORD TO TEACHERS AND DISCUSSION GROUP LEADERS

In using this work as a textbook care needs to be taken that it does not discourage free and lively discussion on the part of the group. Slavish following of a text will stifle lively exchange of thought, for then the end sought by the student is to recite what the text says, rather than to formulate his own opinions and convictions. To avoid this outcome it is suggested that before assigning the material in a particular chapter, the issues first be raised in class discussion. Have the students first of all state their own ideas, or relate what they have been taught concerning a particular question. If the class comprises members from divergent backgrounds, this procedure will usually bring to light differences of opinion within the class itself, and in the clash that ensues students should be encouraged to make the best statements of which they are capable in defense of their respective points of view. It is then that they become aware of their inability to state clearly and forcefully a particular position and, also, of their need for assistance. At this point the need for resource materials is recognized by the student himself and the proper time has come for assigning portions of the text and other collateral reading.

CHAPTER I

Motives for Being Religious

"RELIGION," it is frequently said, "is a very personal matter." Usually, what is meant by this statement is, that religion is an individual concern which each person works out independently for himself, and is too sacred to be shared except with one's intimates. It is a peculiarly personal possession which justifies reticence on the part of the individual and should be so respected by others. True it is that a vital religious faith deals with sacred matters and ought never to be treated with disrespect, but the assumption that each person works out his own religious convictions with little outside help and is not conditioned by his religious environment is open to challenge. There is good reason for thinking that the above familiar remark may frequently be used as a defense mechanism by which a person endeavors to conceal a state of inner uncertainty and confusion which he dislikes to admit and which makes it impossible for him to give expression to a reasonable faith. The probability is that most people credit to themselves much more independence in religious thinking than they ever actually achieve. Some degree of variation from the religious views of parents or associates is interpreted as adequate evidence of having thought things through for oneself, but considered from a broader perspective such a conclusion is found to have little foundation.

THE SOURCES OF RELIGIOUS BELIEFS

An old proverb states, "The apple never falls far from the tree." A strong gust of wind or a rolling slope may carry an apple a little distance from beneath the tree's branches, so that it might affirm, "I am not of the tree." Every observer can easily discern, however, whence the apple came. So it is with our religious beliefs and practices in early life; we do not get far from that which we learned from our families or intimate associates. A child reared in a devout Methodist home may not agree in every respect with his parents' beliefs, but both his beliefs and his ways will much more closely resemble those of his parents than those of a child of a devout Catholic home in the next block. Similarly, the child with a good Catholic rearing cannot think and react like a child of a Quaker community. How much less can a young person of Christian America think like a Hindu of India, or a Buddhist of China, or a Mohammedan of Arabia! For the most part our early beliefs and habits in religion are given to us more or less unconsciously by the social groups in which we grow up, very much as are modes of dress, language, manners, and methods of eating. We are conditioned religiously by early environment just as we are in all other modes of social expression.

Not until we move out into larger circles of life and experience is there much occasion to question the inherited ideas and practices, and in the lives of many persons this happens only to a very limited extent. Most people of the world grow up, live and die in one community, and as long as the prevailing ideas and ways of that community serve them well enough, there is little incentive to change. Even in modern Europe one can find many undisturbed peasant communities where the people live and think in ways almost identical with those of their ancestors for generations back. The same thing is true of isolated communities of America, although the time-span is not so long because of the newness of the country.

STIMULI TO INDEPENDENT THINKING

In the life of the ambitious young American, however, things seldom follow that course. As he grows up his contacts are broadened, and he finds himself thrown into close association with young people of different background and training. He goes to a camp or conference, where young people are gathered from a large area, from communities large and small, from various churches and denominations, and finds that they do not all agree in their ideas about things which he regarded as settled. He finds this disturbing. He goes to college and has a roommate from another city or section of the country, whom he has never seen before. Each craving companionship, they begin to open their inner lives to one another. Then, perhaps, a shock comes. The roommate, a most likeable fellow, does things in all good conscience which our young American has been taught to regard as of the devil. Innocently the one invites the other to participate in that which he has been taught to abhor. Perceiving the latter's discomfiture, the roommate may tend to make light of his conscientious scruples in the matter. In such times one is challenged to rethink his position and to ask himself whether the parental attitude was well founded.

The challenge to rethink one's inherited position may occur in the experience of the classroom. A teacher whose ability is evident and who is endowed with great personal charm is found to take issue with the Biblical account of creation, to advocate the theory of evolution, and to make light of certain traditional teachings of the churches. The student finds himself torn between loyalty to the beliefs of his parents and the minister back home, and his admiration for the apparent learning and convincing arguments of the new teacher. In ways like these the process of independent thinking may be incited, and once started on this course a person may find it impossible ever to regain the dogmatic certainty that characterized the uncritical opinions of his childhood.

IS INDEPENDENT THINKING TO BE DESIRED?

It should not be hastily concluded, however, that independent thinking always results when inherited modes of thought and action are disturbed by wider contacts and new experiences. Oftentimes it happens that people simply substitute one set of ideas for another without submitting either to a real test. Like tramps, they always aim to have the wind at their backs. They lack the courage to head into adverse intellectual currents. Independent thinking is courageous in that it dares to blaze new trails and try out new pathways on one hand, and on the other to stand firm against a veritable tide of popular opinion, if good reason supports the truth of the position. Real independent thinking is rare. In fact, it is by no means generally agreed that independent thinking is desirable in religion, and there are large communions that regard it as highly inimical to the best interests of the religious life. They maintain that the higher truths of religion are given only by direct revelation and transcend human understanding and reason. They must be accepted on the authority of the church, the authorized custodian and interpreter of the revelation. Reason may be exercised properly within the limits of revelation but must never question the truth of the revelation itself. When reason attempts to operate beyond its proper scope it leads not to truth but to error, and imperils the highest religious values. A High-Church Episcopalian has expressed this position in reference to the Creed, as follows:

> The Creed is the Declaration of "The Faith once delivered to the Saints," as revealed by Our Lord, contained in the Scriptures, taught by the Church and set Forth by her Authority. . . . Some of the statements of the Creed are called Holy Mysteries, because they are beyond human understanding, dealing as they do with the Nature or Attributes of God. It is absolutely incumbent upon all persons to believe each and every article of the Creed, as the Church hath declared it, for the denial of any one part of that which God has revealed puts the soul in peril.[1]

The same author in speaking of the church affirms "her authority and not private judgment" to be "the sole judge as to Teaching and Practice." This position tolerates no exercise of private reason that questions the basic assumptions of the faith as expressed in the official creed.

The present writer takes the position that the ability to investigate and reason is an important part of man's divine endowment and can be exercised properly in every realm of life including the most sacred. Progress will be made in religious understanding and in the discovery of spiritual values as men strive after the truth through the clearest and most logical thinking of which they are capable. This is not to deny the fact of revelation, or the coming of truth by sudden flashes of insight. New truth comes more often, perhaps, through intuitive insights than through following out syllogisms, but if these insights stand they must receive the confirmation of good reason. Moreover, the new flashes of truth come usually to those who already possess a high degree of understanding in the particular realm, not to the ignorant.

Ideas and attitudes received as a portion of a person's social heritage

---

[1] A. C. Knowles: *The Practice of Religion*, 4th Edition, p. 13. Edwin S. Gorham. New York, 1911.

may be good or bad, constructive or baneful, but they are not personal judgments arrived at through the exercise of individual reason. Most youthful religious beliefs, and those of most adults also, are essentially contributions to their minds of the society in which they live and are not individual judgments arrived at through critical thinking. Even in the case of a good many whose ideas have undergone change, what has happened has been but the substitution of one set of ideas and attitudes for another, not as a result of carefully weighing the arguments in the case, but because the new set involves less conflict with the prevailing intellectual current or surrounding social practice of a new social environment. In such cases it is conceivable that a lower set of beliefs may be substituted for a higher, as well as the opposite, or a less wholesome social practice put in the place of a better one. There is good reason for thinking that the latter happens not infrequently when young people break home ties and establish themselves in new situations, whether in college, business or marriage. They yield to new social pressures, perhaps reluctantly, but nonetheless surely, not because reasoned judgment approves the new way as better, but because it takes too much courage to stand against the tide of thought and practice in a new community. At the same time these occasions offer opportunities for real emancipation through the exercise of personal judgment. In such situations one may find incentives for independent thinking. For the assistance of those who choose to pursue this more courageous course with reference to religious problems books like this one are written, not to dominate, but to help clarify the issues and the alternatives.

WHY ARE PEOPLE RELIGIOUS?

It is one thing to discover the source of a person's religious beliefs and reactions and another thing to know why he continues to be religious. The source of people's religion is their social inheritance, as has been shown, but what are the incentives that operate to keep them devoted to it? To find a sufficient answer to that question it will not be enough to face a great many people with the question, "Why are you religious?" and catalogue the answers. Among the important revelations of modern psychology is that one which declares that very frequently persons are not aware of their own motives in action. The impelling urges often belong to the realm of the unconscious and are realized at the point of consciousness but dimly, if at all. The conscious mind may readily furnish rationalizations of conduct, but these may be far afield from the real forces determining behavior. When asked why they pursue a particular course of action, people may be ready with a number of good answers, but objective examination might reveal that the real motives were quite different from explanations offered. This does not mean that those who gave mistaken answers were hypocrites, but simply that they themselves were not aware of their real motives in action. This is very apt to be true with respect to religious activity, and one may learn more about actual motives by observing the conduct of people in various situations than by asking direct questions. Such observation will bring to light a number of reasons that operate to make people religious.

POPULAR MOTIVES

A great many people engage in religious activity simply because it is considered the thing to do in the social group in which their lives are cast. Social pressures tend to make us all conform to that which the particular society considers right and proper, to that which is deemed commendable or highly respectable. To act otherwise is to court disfavor, and if the breach with established custom is at all marked, it invites ostracism. It is characteristic of human nature "to want to belong," to stand well among one's fellows, to secure social approbation and avoid disapproval. It is this particular urge, especially strong in young people, that makes them the easy victims of passing fads. In the writer's high-school days every senior felt constrained to wear a derby hat. Without a derby, at least on dress-up occasions, he felt very self-conscious, and was sure that everyone looked down on him with pity that he should be so lacking in an essential of propriety. The remembrance only provokes a smile now, but it was serious business then. So it is with every generation. We all want to do that which commands respect and social approval, and herein lies the dominant reason why many people engage in the activities of religion. Their society demands it as a condition of approval.

Religion which is motivated merely by the demand for respectability and social approval does not go very deep into one's nature, and like a cloak it may easily be set aside if one encounters a different social climate. Transplant such a person into a new environment where he associates with another social group with different interests and standards of judgment, and the former interest in religion may soon fade out, if the new community happens to be indifferent or hostile to religion. Those in position to observe young people breaking with their home communities and entering the new environment of college witness frequent examples of this fact. It is not at all uncommon, as any minister to students can testify, for a student who was very active in the home church, the leader of the young people's society, perhaps, and the pride of the pastor, to act after arriving on a college campus as if he never had had any religious connections. Why the change? Simply this, at home to be a leader in the activities of the church was the most direct route to recognition and honor. In college the student found himself in a different atmosphere where the same course of action was indifferently regarded or made the subject of ridicule by the new social group. All of us worship more or less at the shrine of the God of Recognition, and many people are so enamored of this idol that they will do anything to curry his favor. They will be enthusiastically religious in one place and in one group, and become utterly indifferent in the next. Perhaps they are unable to understand their own reactions. They may excuse their indifference by stating that the minister is uninteresting, or by saying that the music is poor and the service is unattractive; but the objective observer perceives that the determining factor is the desire to gain personal recognition and social approval, and to avoid their opposites.

A second motive which operates to make people religious is the fear of consequences, if they should dare to live otherwise. This cause is not functioning nearly as effectively in the present age as it has in generations past, when eloquent evangelists painted lurid pictures of the sufferings of the damned. Pictures of heavenly bliss were never half as convincing as a foretaste of the undying flames of hell. Men were made to shudder with horror at the prospect which threatened them and gladly grasped that which promised salvation from bitter and enduring agony. The experience of salvation was like the joy of climbing into a lifeboat when shipwrecked and about to drown in the unplumbed depths of a cruel sea.

It will always be important for man to face realistically the inevitable and natural consequences of unsocial or sinful action, and later in this work attention will be directed to this end. But it is a great boon that the older method of trying to make men religious by striking terror into their hearts and minds is passing away. Fear is a necessary human motive, but it is a low motive and taken by itself it leads one into a craven sort of life. One's desires prompt him to a certain course of action, but he refrains from doing the thing he wants to do because of fear. The evil way of life is regarded as much more enticing and interesting than the good, but should you dare to satisfy those natural desires in this world, woe be unto you both in this world and throughout the world to come. If you give yourself to enjoyment here in this brief span of earthly life, you can expect to suffer torment throughout eternity. Therefore, if you are prudent, you will stoically refrain from doing the things you would like to do. Or more than likely you will approach as near the restricted territory as you dare without actually trespassing, or you may even furtively reach over and nibble the forbidden fruit, wanting to take a real bite, but afraid to do so. As for religion, you are not drawn to it for its own sake, but you contract for enough of it to insure you against the sufferings that await sinners. Such a view of life is tragically fallacious and represents a travesty on the real nature of righteousness, but it still persists in some quarters and many people are moved by such considerations. At its best it is not an exalted motive for being religious.

A third motive that moves people to take stock in religion is that of expediency. Much of life still lies beyond the limits of human control and understanding, and in the experience of all there are times when life seems too much for us. We do not always ride the crest of the waves. Sometimes the billows overwhelm us. In such times it is well to be in good standing with those superhuman forces which may presumably come to our aid and help us over the crisis. It is well to establish a little moral reserve or spiritual credit against the day of misfortune and it is the function of religion to provide this reserve. Sometimes students, who take their work none too seriously during the semester and find themselves near the brink of disaster at examination time, turn to prayer in the hope of enlisting the favor of the Almighty to the end of securing a magical deliverance from their deserved plight.

That God may be indulgent in such an hour of need it is well to court his favor. Just so, many people find it advisable to keep on sufficiently good terms with religious institutions to justify turning to religion for help in times of personal crisis when the demands of life seem too much for them. This is not to say that religion should not function in such occasions, nor that it is not fitting to pray in such circumstances, but when religion is regarded as a resource to be drawn upon only in times of personal insufficiency, it is largely a matter of expediency.

A fourth motive that operates to turn some people to religion is the desire for an escape from the difficult, disagreeable, hard and sordid realities of life. Some people lack the courage to face life's vicissitudes, or are irked by its annoyances, or do not get along well with their fellow men, and they would flee from the hard facts and seek escape in some dream world where all is beautiful and serene, and where nothing ever happens to disturb the calm of one's soul. Religion affords an opportunity for flight into an ideal world of fancy where for the time being one finds release from arduous responsibilities and becomes oblivious to his troubles. Such people do not like stirring sermons that are designed to move people to action, or that challenge them to take up the cudgels against destructive evils in society. They want to hear only religion's comforting words and blessed assurances, and to be soothed by sweet music and the soft glow of stained-glass windows. Religion for them is not a means of discovering and relating themselves to deep realities of life which incite fresh vision and bring new courage with which to face the problems of daily living. It is an escape from reality, and as such is enervating rather than invigorating; it ministers to cowardice rather than courage, and counsels retreat from life's problems instead of direct attack upon them. Such religion is properly characterized by the Marxist formula as "the opiate of the people."

All of the motives thus far described, when evaluated, must be put down as of themselves inadequate, if not improper incentives, for being religious. In the light of this fact we must ask whether there is a sufficient, reasonable and adequate motive for living religiously. It is easier to assert that there is such a motive than to state it. But that there is such a motive we may confidently affirm. It is itself a composite and may be expressed in various ways.

AN ADEQUATE MOTIVE

We shall endeavor to approach it from several different angles. The intelligent man recognizes that there are low levels and high levels of human experience. He perceives that life is characterized by potentialities and high possibilities as yet unrealized in experience. The intelligently religious man finds an adequate motive in the desire and purpose to actualize those high possibilities in the life of society about him. If we think in terms of the significance of lives, we recognize that some are of little consequence to society, some of evil significance, and others of great significance in the realm of the good. The intelligent religious man is religious because he desires to invest his life with the largest possible meaning for the better life of the world. If we make the approach from the standpoint of values, we recognize that some characters are base and others noble, in terms of the values which they cherish and the aspirations which move them. As between high values and low, the intelligently religious person seeks to devote himself to life's highest and most abiding values. It is of the very nature of religion to assume that there are values, causes, or loyalties in the world which justify complete devotion on the part of men, and the very essence of religious experience is for man to yield to the claim of such a loyalty which is so much more important than himself that he willingly gives himself in consecration to it. To one who loses self in a great devotion life takes on larger dimensions, and the truth becomes evident that the abundant life is found through the loss of self in a great consecration.

In his quest for the abundant life for himself and his fellows the religious man will not hide his face or seek to run away from reality. He seeks escape only from the domination of surface or superficial aspects of reality which perforce occupy the center of his attention so much of the time. He endeavors to build his life on a foundation more secure than the passing flux of the average man's daily round. Through the means of worship he seeks to relate his life to the fundamental purpose moving within the universe so that his individual striving may be in complete harmony with the deep moving currents of life. By such adjustment to life's deeper realities he seeks to avoid frustration and defeat, and to attain a sense of fulfillment and triumph. Through alliance with these deeper realities he endeavors to make himself the instrument of powers greater than himself that enable him to achieve with a power beyond his own in behalf of the great cause to which he has committed himself.

Herein then is the adequate motive for religious living, the desire to actualize high possibilities in the realm of the good and the true and the beautiful, to live significantly in relation to the social process, to build upon deep reality, to be the instrument of great forces beyond one's own strength, and so to realize in company with others the abundant life. Devotion to religion on such grounds affects character more deeply than the requirements of social recognition. It is far more positive than fear, and far more adventurous than expediency, and instead of fleeing from reality it seeks out and builds upon the deepest and most fundamental of truths. Such is the avenue to fullness and richness of life for mankind.

CHAPTER II

The Nature and Functions
of Religion

ATTEMPTS to define religion have been legion and little would be gained by endeavoring to add another definition to the existing confusion. A few observations, however, may help to clear the atmosphere and bring the writer and reader together on a common ground of understanding. In their endeavor to locate the most essential aspect of this phenomenon various writers have endeavored to state the essence of religion in terms of one or another of the familiar aspects of mental experience. There are those who would base religion almost exclusively in the emotions, others in the intellect, and still others in activities of the will. The first group finds the basis of religion in emotional experiences. It may be subdivided according to the nature of the feelings which are emphasized. Some would say that religion takes its rise in an emotional upheaval, in which the feeling of being out of joint with life is superseded by the sense of proper adjustment and harmony with the forces of destiny. Others affirm that religion expresses itself in an emotional glow that gives radiance to life, or in a zest for living, or in a fervor for an ideal or worthy cause. For others religion arises in a feeling of personal insufficiency, which in turn causes one to realize his dependence upon the superior forces of life and results in an attitude of submissiveness to some higher power or powers. Schleiermacher, famed as the father of nineteenth century theology, defined religion as "the feeling of absolute dependence." In still other circles as ancient as the Dionysiac revels of early Thrace, or as modern as holiness or Pentecostal groups, the essence of the matter has been a heightened feeling of personal power produced by inducing states of great emotional excitement in which the participant senses union of self with the Divine. In all these cases the root of the matter is located in the emotional life.

Members of another division consider religion as the product of intellectual activity that yields certain convictions about the nature of life and human destiny. Religion is essentially belief. Its most characteristic expressions are found in doctrines, creeds, or confessions of faith. Every religion is characterized by a body of dogma, and religions can be classified according to the degree of intellectual enlightenment evident in their doctrines, some being high religions and others low. The religious person, according to this view, is one who accepts as his own the official body of dogma by giving intellectual assent thereto. The non-religious man is the heretic, one who rejects the acknowledged creed of the particular religious system. Not the nature or quality of emotional experience is the proper test with this group, but soundness in the faith, or doctrinal correctness.

A third group thinks of religion in volitional terms, primarily as an approved mode of action. Religion is a way of life. The required practices may vary from prescribed rituals or ceremonials on the one hand, to highly moral acts of mercy and altruism in the social sphere on the other. A religion is known by its practices systematized into ceremonial or moral codes, and the religious person is one who conforms his mode of life to these requirements. He frequents the temple, synagogue, mosque, church or shrine; he offers sacrifices, makes offerings, engages in expiations, prays, gives alms to the poor, visits the sick, feeds the hungry, clothes the naked, relieves distress, mourns with those in sorrow and rejoices with those who are glad, according to the requirements of the code of action of the particular religion. These acts may or may not be accompanied by stimulated emotions, and the performer may or may not comprehend the dogmas of the faith, but the one essential is conformity to prescribed religious practices.

A BALANCED VIEW

To one who finds it possible to take something of an objective attitude toward the various expressions of religion it becomes evident that the essence of the matter is not to be found by selecting one of these reactions to the exclusion of the others, but rather through effecting a synthesis of them. Religion cannot be defined adequately in terms of emotional reactions alone, nor as a system of beliefs alone, nor as a way of life alone. All of these are valid and essential expressions of the religious impulse, and religion at its best unites them all in a harmonious and balanced whole. The Gospel of John represents Jesus as declaring, "I am the way, the truth, and the life." The full orb of religion cannot be described in less terms than these. Religion affects the whole life of man and cannot be related exclusively to any one aspect of experience.

Not only is religion not to be confined to one aspect of experience exclusively, but the highest type of religion maintains a balance between these modes of expression. Over-emphasis on one element at the expense of the others tends to produce vagaries ranging from dangerous fanaticisms on the one hand to lifeless forms on the other. Religion without emotion lacks dynamic. The power house of personality is established in the emotions. So far as releasing energy in effective action is concerned the depth of one's feeling about a matter is of more importance than how one thinks. Without feeling, religion lacks warmth of spirit and radiance. It becomes anæmic. But religion which is all emotion is fanaticism. It is divorced from practical ends and has fulfilled its function in heightened feelings. It is simply a method of going on an emotional spree. When the fervor abates, exhaustion follows, and the devotee is less ready to meet the demands and trials of life than before.

Religion requires intelligence for its highest functioning. Intelligence must direct its energies to worth-while ends by discovering the values worthy of devotion. Man cannot live rightly unless he thinks rightly. If he is to think correctly his thinking must be founded upon basic truths about the nature of man and the world which he inhabits. There are a good many debated questions in life about which it makes little difference what the average person believes. But there are other questions concerning which it makes great difference what one thinks. There are "beliefs that matter." It does not make much difference what an ordinary person thinks about the composition of the moon or on the question of whether or not Mars is inhabited. But it does make a difference what people believe is a justification for murder, or of what honesty and honor consist. Although somewhat more removed from immediately practical concerns, it makes a tremendous difference from the standpoint of a complete life whether one believes this to be a God-ruled world, or a Godless world. It makes a difference what one believes about the character of God, whether he is perfectly righteous and trustworthy, or whether he is whimsical and capricious. It makes a difference whether God loves men, or is indifferent to them, or regards them as only puppets for his enjoyment. It makes a difference whether one believes that a moral order expresses itself in this world, or whether our differentiations between right and wrong are mere human expedients without any basis in the structure of things. It makes a difference for life what men believe about the nature of human destiny. It is the business of religion to supply the highest possible truths in answer to these important queries and the task is one that calls for the exercise of the highest intelligence. If the emotions represent the power plant, then the intellect represents the pilot who should set the course that life shall take, that the energies of life be devoted to reasonable ends. When, however, religion exhausts itself in finding reasonable answers to difficult questions, it is cold and lifeless, and attractive only to those who enjoy mental gymnastics. It is powerless to redeem a person caught in the grip of evil habit, or to remake an evil society.

To effect the connection between the guidance of the intellect and the energies of the emotions there must be an act of will in the form of a commitment of life to a practical program designed to give realization to the values which intelligence reveals as possibilities. Religion to be complete must express itself in ethical standards—in a program of action, and in a practical way of life. Through persistent and active devotion to the ideals which religion on the intellectual side approves, the emotions become conditioned to the support of these ends. But religion that exhausts itself in conformity to a ready-made mode of life, not undergirded by intellectual conviction, nor infused with emotional dynamic, will prove shallow and without meaning. It will become a wearisome burden to be borne, or a distasteful duty to be performed, without zest or saving power. Religion at its best must relate itself to the total life of man.

IN TERMS OF ENDS AND MEANS

It should be possible to go further than has been done thus far in this discourse in characterizing this phenomenon which we have found relates itself to all aspects of life. In the judgment of the present writer religion may best be described in terms of the ends which it seeks and the means used in their attainment. Religion always seeks the realization of high values, apprehended by man as possibilities and interpreted as expressions of the divine will, but only partially realized in experience. The values sought vary greatly with the state of life and the state of existing culture. The wants of primitive man which he seeks to satisfy by religious means are quite elemental, such as the desire for adequate food and shelter, physical protection from mysterious dangers lurking in the environment, and sex satisfaction. As civilization advances, man's knowledge of his world increases and he learns ways of meeting these elemental needs by his own powers with the result that they become less the objects of religious quest. But newer and higher wants take their places. Man becomes aware of new possibilities of life hitherto undreamed of. The new values will probably be more intangible than the old, such as the desire for understanding, for affection, for an appreciation of beauty in nature, music, and art, for intellectual fellowship, or for personal righteousness. With the growing knowledge of the importance of social relations the new values become more social in nature, such as the desire for a better society, for a warless world, for a brotherhood of races, for the Kingdom of God. In any case religion is concerned with a quest for values recognized as highly desirable but as yet beyond man's unaided power of achievement.

All activities of life represent efforts to realize desirable ends, but not all means of securing values are properly religious. There are secular as well as religious means of seeking ends in life. Religion as a method is characterized by its particular reference. It seeks its ends through adjustment to more-than-human powers upon which the achievement of the desired values is believed to depend. The higher power may be conceived as a multitude of invisible spirits that infest the immediate natural environment, as in the case of primitive men, or it may be visualized as a personal god of supreme power and righteousness, as among Jews and Christians. It may be conceived as an impersonal moral order, like the Heaven-Order of Confucianism, or Karma, the inexorable law of moral retribution, as found in the religions of India. In a religion characterized by a high degree of nationalism, the spirit of the nation may be regarded as the power which orders destiny. Among the philosophic minded a cosmic process making for the creation of beauty and worth in the world may be the essential factor. The form may be variously conceived, but always the method of religion is that of bringing life into harmonious adjustment with the will, purpose, ways, modes of action, or ongoing process of that power or powers upon whose action the attainment of the desired ends is believed ultimately to depend. The working out of this relationship may result in activities of an educational, political, economic, medical, or other social nature, ways of action secular when taken by themselves, but religious when guided and determined by what is conceived to be the requirement of that higher power to which men seek adjustment. In Christianity, for example, the guiding factor will be the will and purpose of God as that is revealed to men supremely in the character and mission of Jesus Christ. Through adjustment to the divine will made manifest in Christ men seek fullness of life. In Buddhism through adjustment to the law of Karma by freeing the soul of all material attachment and specific desire, the quester hopes for escape from the necessity of continued life in many rebirths, for deliverance from the grief and burden of living, and for the attainment of that blissful quiescent state known as Nirvana. The ends sought and the specific means are quite different, but the essential method is the same, that of adjustment to the requirements of a higher power which determines destiny. It is this reference which distinguishes religion from other techniques of securing values.

PRACTICAL CONTRIBUTIONS TO LIFE

If one were to collect the testimony of religious people concerning the practical contributions which religion had made to their lives he would soon have an extended and imposing list. There would be no general agreement, in fact a great deal of disagreement, as to what things should be put down to the credit of religion, but if one accepted all the statements of religious devotees there would not be a boon or good of any kind that would be left out. It may be valuable, however, to review some of the contributions most frequently mentioned in the testimony of religious people:

Provides comfort in the hour of sorrow.

Affords guidance in meeting the issues of life.
Releases from fears.
Ministers to hope.
Increases the joy of living.
Heightens moral courage.
Refreshes drooping spirits.
Affords moral cleansing.
Illuminates the problems of life.
Challenges to adventure.
Increases personal power.
Affords superhuman help in the time of man's insufficiency.
Sustains in event of crisis.
Contributes to poise.
Induces serenity.
Ministers to health or healing.
Increases wealth.
Makes friendships richer.
Enables one to live in rich fellowship with the Divine.
Heightens æsthetic appreciations.
Stimulates the quest for truth.
Undergirds morality with spiritual sanctions.
Promises eternal life.
Provides a scale of values.
Invests life with meaning.
Integrates personality around a high purpose.
Enables one to live with a sense of mission.
Affords redemption from evil habits and appetites.
Stimulates unselfishness.
Breaks down barriers between nationalities, races, and classes.
Inspires movements for the relief of human misery and suffering.
Serves as a spur to advances in human culture.
Increases moral sensitivity.
Makes men aware of sins and evils to be combated.

If now we should turn the tables and ask the enemies of religion to bring in their testimony, we should find that they would charge religion with the exact opposite of everything credited to it by its devotees and perhaps would be able to supply examples in every instance. They would charge religion with every crime in the catalogue of human evils from individual and mass murder to the worst of sexual perversions.

Again they would be able to furnish evidence from the annals of human history. The indictments would have to be admitted and the evidence accepted. Not all forms and expressions of religion have been wholesome, nor have all contributed to human welfare. Perverted or unbalanced religion is without doubt a dangerous force. The preponderance of evidence, however, is on the side of the constructive contributions of intelligent religion and on this basis religion is entitled to an important place among the factors contributing to the development of human culture.

BASIC FUNCTIONS

Of the many contributions credited to religion some are evidently contingent upon the truth of others; or, in other words, some are fundamental and others secondary. It will greatly simplify the situation and further our understanding if the more fundamental functions of religion can be separated from the rest. It would be impossible to secure general agreement as to what constitutes the primary functions of religion. We shall be near to the heart of the matter, however, if we say that a major function of religion is to reveal life's essential meaning. There are those who would say that the major function of religion is to infuse life with meaning, but on the basis of the nature of religion heretofore described in this chapter, the assumption is that there is already meaning in life, which has its origin in the purpose of God for theistic religions, or in the program of destiny for non-theistic religions. The business of religion accordingly is not so much to create meaning as to reveal the meaning already present. Life without meaning would be intolerable. All of us are aware of many lesser meanings in the great variety of human activities, but the crucial question concerns the meaning of the whole. Is there a central meaning which gathers into itself all lesser meanings and gives them permanent validity? Or is life at its center without meaning and all our human values temporary and ephemeral? As Dean Robert Russell Wicks affirms, sooner or later men are driven back to ask the question, "What is the Reason for Living?"—and no more fundamental question can be asked. Man does not need to comprehend the full meaning of existence in order to keep up the struggle, but he needs the assurance that life is characterized by a worth-while meaning. Convince him that life is without a comprehensive and significant meaning and you will rob him of his deepest incentive. It is the business of religion to make clear the operation of meaning in existence and as far as possible throw light on the nature and substance of that meaning.

One of the things that should flow out from the discovery of life's central meaning should be light on the whole problem of relative values. All life represents a questing for ends conceived by persons to be desirable. But there is a wide difference of opinion as to what are important and unimportant ends or what constitute the higher and lower values of life. Through even partial knowledge of the principal end of existence the important values to be sought in life should become clear, for they will be those in fullest accord with the great end of the total process. To the extent that religion succeeds in gaining an understanding of the meaning of life, it should enable man to establish a trustworthy scale of values by which to guide his own pursuits, aiding him to pass by the inconsequential, the fallacious, and ephemeral, in favor of the more rewarding and abiding. Religion should function, therefore, as a guide to moral endeavor.

Growing out of the two functions already discussed follows another of foremost importance for effective living, that of integrating the life of the individual about some great absorbing end or purpose. There will be great variety of individual purposes in life as the abilities, talents, aptitudes, and circumstances of life vary. But they will all find their validation in the contribution they make to life's central meaning and to the building up of its highest values. It is the business of religion to help each individual to evolve his own purpose in living and to organize his abilities and energies into the most effective support of that purpose. Such integration is the pathway to an effective and satisfying life. Life's great joys are the by-products of significant achievement in the carrying forward of a worthy purpose.

One of the most important ways in which religion mediates its blessings to life is through the fellowship of religious people. Through such a fellowship the individual of insufficient resources to stand alone against adverse currents of moral temptation or the tendency to despair finds himself supported and sustained and is enabled to face life with courage and confidence. To establish the individual within the supporting fellowship of a spiritual community is an important function of religion.

In the light of what has been said about the particular method of religion in attaining its values, one of its major functions is that of bringing to men a sense of fellowship with the Divine. It should bring them a sense of harmonious adjustment to that greater-than-human power upon whom the issues of destiny finally depend. From this relationship he should gain access to power, sufficient to help him meet successfully all the vicissitudes of life and avoid frustration in living. This does not mean that life will always proceed smoothly in every detail for the religious man; nor does it assure the breaking down of all resistance, nor the banishment of all trouble. On the other hand it does mean, however, that instead of having to contend constantly against a rising tide of opposition, man should live with the sense of being carried forward by the main current of life, and of being in league with powers that uphold him instead of beat him down. Religion should enable a man to enter into alliance with powers greater than himself.

Given these things, an introduction to the meaning of life, a scale of moral values, integration of individual life about some worthy purpose, membership in a religious community and an alliance with spiritual forces of the universe, the many lesser contributions of religion to life should follow in experience as naturally as the beauties of nature respond to the presence of the sun and rain.

CHAPTER III

Will Science Displace Religion?

ARE science and religion two different ways of approaching the same problems of life, or are they concerned with quite different ends? If they are two different ways of approaching the same problems, then there is good reason, in light of the remarkable achievements of science in recent generations, to believe that it will displace religion. Some people would have us think of religion as a mode of dealing with the universe that was developed prior to science, and, now that a better method is being developed, it will gradually be displaced as science completes and perfects itself. But if these two disciplines are concerned with different ends and goals, then there is no ground for fear that one will succeed in banishing the other, for they will complement one another.

SCIENCE AND RELIGION IN CONFLICT

A bitter conflict has been waged between the findings of science about the universe and certain traditional religious ideas. The warfare has been of rather long duration, dying down in certain generations but flaring up with new zeal in others. For the most part the views of the world upheld by religion have not come off well in this conflict, for wherever they have been opposed to well-established findings of science they have been forced to yield eventually to the truth of the scientific position.

Some of the most important battles in this warfare have been stimulated particularly by progress in the science of astronomy. The Christian religion very naturally formulated itself in terms of the ancient world-view which prevailed generally in Biblical times. The universe as then conceived was a relatively simple affair. It consisted of a flat earth which apparently was surrounded by water on all sides and underneath as well. Over the earth and supported by it was a solid firmament, above which water was again to be found, and above the celestial waters was heaven and the abode of God. There were shutters in the firmament which when opened by divine decree permitted the water from above the firmament to pour through the openings and to descend in the form of rain upon the earth. God had also fixed certain luminaries within the firmament which shed their light upon the earth, the sun which moved across the firmament by day, and the stars by night. The natural forces of the earth were controlled very largely by the direct activity or decrees of the Deity. With the development of astronomy, men came to conceive of planets circulating in the heavens, and there followed the development of the Ptolemaic theory. This held, however, to the earth as the center of the universe and did not seem to require much change in the thought of men concerning the relation of God to the world, although it did conflict in some respects with the world-view contained in the Bible.

In the sixteenth century under the leadership of Copernicus, a much more revolutionary theory was proposed, namely that the sun rather than the earth was the center of the universe, and that our earth was a subsidiary of the sun revolving about it in company with other planets rather than the earth as a center with the sun revolving about it for the earth's particular benefit. This was much more critical from the standpoint of religion, not only because it was contrary to the world-view set forth in the Bible, but it seemed greatly to diminish the importance of our earth. Jealous of the importance of the earth and of man's place in the scheme of things, the church rose to the defense of the older world-view and invoked the horrors of the inquisition against those who dared to deny the truth of the Bible in this regard. But truth was on the side of science and religion had to yield eventually and to adapt its views to this more complex universe. Since the sixteenth century it has had, of course, to re-adapt its views many times over as the boundaries of the known universe were pushed out beyond the power of human imagination to conceive, and our particular solar system was found to be a very minor system in a seemingly limitless number of solar systems that comprise one galaxy included in a galaxy of galaxies.

In recent generations an equally serious controversy has raged over the issue of evolution. This was precipitated by the publication of Darwin's *Origin of Species* in 1859, which marshaled an abundant evidence in support of the theory that the higher forms of life, including man, had developed through a long series of changes from simple and low forms of life. This theory denied that man was created directly by the hand of God who had breathed into him the breath of life. It seemed to many to deny altogether the fact of divine creation and to lead to the conclusion that man was not made in the image of God but was little higher than the beast from which he had emerged. This seemed to rob man of his dignity and to debase that which religion exalted. The institutions of religion set themselves for defense against this new assault upon the dignity of man, but as science has been able to accumulate a massive amount of evidence from a variety of fields in support of the thesis, the principle has come to be generally accepted as fact and religion has had to adjust to this principle as an accepted truth. In the adjustment man has not forfeited his dignity.

Despite the seriousness of these discoveries for prevailing religious beliefs of the times, the fact remains that religion has been able to adapt itself to these and many other disturbing findings of science without any real loss to religion itself. As Rabbi Abba Hillel Silver has expressed it, "Religion, tied to the dead body of antiquated scientific notions, was tragically handicapped." Though the disassociation has been a painful operation, religion has gained in the process.

In view of the seriousness of these controversies in the past, is it reasonable to expect that the future relations of these two disciplines will continue to be marked by bitter conflict? Surely science is destined to continue its discoveries of new facts about life and the world which will cause us to revise many of our accepted views about the nature of things. It is likely that there always will be a certain amount of tension between the statements of religion and the newer findings of science, because religious convictions are always expressed in terms of the existing world-view at the time of their formulation. The religious insight so expressed may be essentially sound although the world-view changes. Calling in question the older scientific view seems also to involve the religious insights expressed in terms of that older view. In time the abiding religious truth comes to be restated in terms acceptable to the newer scientific truth and the tension relaxes. Thus tensions will appear every time new findings of science seem to jeopardize religious values. But inasmuch as new scientific discoveries create tensions between various fields of science and schools of scientific thought this should be no cause for alarm.

Granting that a certain degree of tension is inevitable, the question remains will it be necessary to engage in life-and-death struggles like those of the past in order to accomplish the necessary readjustments. The answer to that question will depend very largely on the attitudes of religious and scientific men. Men of science must take care not to draw conclusions from their findings that take them out of their own field. When the man of science speaks as a scientist his words should be accorded reasonable authority, but when he speaks as a philosopher his findings may be open to question. There is no justification, therefore, for scientists to assume dogmatic attitudes about the meaning of science for other realms of life. Likewise religious men must cease to be dogmatic about matters that properly belong to the sphere of science. Religion's dogmatism in the past is easily explained in view of the belief that religion was in possession of a divine revelation, the full truth of which was supernaturally guaranteed. To question any aspect of the revelation was equivalent to questioning the knowledge and veracity of God. If religion continues to insist on the superiority of its revelations to truth in any realm obtained by other means, it is undoubtedly destined for more serious trouble in the future. If, however, religion will regard its own insights and convictions as partial truths to be held tentatively until fuller light comes and will anticipate the coming of fuller knowledge about the nature of things, it should be able to make the necessary adjustments with a minimum of friction. If religion can join science in holding its present conclusions as tentative propositions to be revised in the light of fuller knowledge, the relationship that will characterize these two interests in the future will not be that of bitter enmity, but rather of friendly adjustment.

The question may be raised whether religious convictions held as tentative conclusions will command the same devotion from men as when put forwarrd as dogmatic certainties. There is no good reason why they should not, particularly when it is realized that new and higher truths are revealed only to those who are willing to act on the basis of present understanding whether in the field of science or religion. New truth may be revolutionary in its effects but is never fully divorced from what has gone before. The discovery of truth usually follows a sequence and the last discovery would not be possible except as the preceding one had already been established. There is no valid reason, therefore, for withholding devotion from accepted religious truths because they may be modified in the future.

THE FUNCTIONS COMPARED

The heart of our problem in answering the question, will science displace religion, as suggested in the opening paragraph of the chapter, is the matter of the respective functions of these two interests. If they minister to the same needs of the human spirit, then it is to be expected that the more efficient will supersede the other; but if they serve different needs then we may find that they complement one another and are mutually dependent. In the latter case they must develop together and there are good reasons for thinking that the latter relationship prevails. There is an increasing disposition on the part of scientists and religious leaders alike to recognize the necessity and interdependence of these two approaches to life. Let science go as far as it can in forwarding its own researches, religion will continue to have necessary and vital functions to perform which science alone could never render. Let us examine the functions of these two disciplines.

Science is both segmented and partial in its approach to reality. There is no science of the whole, only particular sciences which make their respective contributions to the common fund of knowledge. A particular science stakes out a claim for itself in the vast domain of human knowledge, and having determined the boundaries of its field, it seeks to exploit that area for facts. The method used combines observation, gathering of data, analysis, experimentation, classification and generalization. There is overlapping, of course, among the sciences and a large degree of interdependence. Mathematics is a basic analytical science and all other sciences make use of its techniques. Physics and chemistry are basic descriptive sciences and are closely related to each other in their common interest in the structure of matter, but at other points they diverge widely. The biological sciences could not exist without chemistry and the social sciences cannot disregard the biological sciences such as genetics, physiology and psychology. But interdependent as they are there is no science of the whole of reality, only a series of sciences which make their specific contributions to the fund of human knowledge.

Science is also partial with respect to the kind of knowledge which it seeks to establish. This partiality is exercised toward those facts of life that lend themselves readily to quantitative analysis such as weight, measurement and number. It is interested only in the quantitative aspect of qualitative matters, as in wave-lengths and wave-patterns of musical tones. To diagram the appearance and frequency of particular sound waves is not to describe by any means the full reality of beautiful music. As valuable as that knowledge is for musicians and makers of musical instruments, it is partial knowledge of the total reality of the experience. The aim of science is accurate description but it deals only with certain abstracted elements of experience and reduces its findings to what J. Arthur Thomson calls "intellectual shorthand formulæ describing uniformities of sequence." Formulæ are useful instruments of thought and understanding, but no formula can describe completely the total reality of any human experience. The same authority says, "Science always knows in part and prophesies in part. Its method is by abstraction; that is to say, it seeks to focus attention on certain aspects or properties at a time. The geologist does not as such leave any room for the *beauty* of the scenery, yet the fact of beauty may be as real a part of his experience as a knowledge of petrography."[1]

Canon B. H. Streeter is the author of a classic illustration of the partiality of scientific knowledge. If, he says, he wished to tell a friend who had never been there of the city of Venice he might show him a plan of the city. The plan would be an accurate description of one aspect of the city. But if he wished to give his friend some idea of the beauty and attractiveness of Venice, he would show him Turner's famous picture. The map of the city would represent scientific knowl-

[1] J. Arthur Thomson, *Science and Religion*, p. 13 f. Scribners, 1925.

edge, the picture other kinds of knowledge that lie outside the province of science. Both are required if knowledge is to approximate completeness.[2]

Summing up the function of science Sir Arthur Thomson says: "It seeks to answer the question: *What is this? Whence is it? How does it come to be as it is, and how does it continue in being?* and sometimes *Whither Away?* as when we contemplate an evolving species or a dying star. But science as science never asks the question *Why?* That is to say, it never inquires into the meaning, or significance, or purpose of this manifold Being, Becoming, and Having Been. This is not its métier."

In the limitation of science thus evident an intimation is given of the necessity of religion serving as a complement to science for the understanding of life. As indicated in the preceding chapter religion is concerned to discover life's inner meanings, its highest values, and its ultimate destiny. Its approach to reality is not segmented, but to life as a whole, in the effort to discover the totality of meaning from which all particular concerns gain their significance. This desire to know life's inner meaning, its goal, and its values is just as insistent and important to human minds as the urge to know the facts about life.

The complementary relationship of these two interests is abundantly attested by the declarations of men of science. In such a matter the testimony of so eminent a scientist as Albert Einstein should be of special interest. Before a conference of representatives of theological schools held at Princeton in 1939 and reported in *Information Service* published by the Federal Council of Churches he made the following assertions in the course of his address:

The scientific method can teach us nothing beyond how facts are related to, and conditioned by, each other. The aspiration toward such objective knowledge belongs to the highest of which man is capable, and you will certainly not suspect me of wishing to belittle the achievements and the heroic efforts of man in this sphere. Yet it is equally clear that knowledge of what *is* does not open the door directly to what *should be*. One can have the clearest and most complete knowledge of what *is,* and yet not be able

[2] *Reality*, p. 31, Macmillan, 1927.

to deduct from that what should be the *goal* of our human aspirations. Objective knowledge provides us with powerful instruments for the achievement of certain ends, but the ultimate goal itself and the longing to reach it must come from another source. And it is hardly necessary to argue for the view that our existence and our activity acquire meaning only by setting up of such a goal and of corresponding values. . . .

To make clear these fundamental ends and valuations, and to set them fast in the emotional life of the individual, seems to me precisely the most important function which religion has to perform in the social life of man.

We may also call to witness an eminent scientist in the person of Julian Huxley, who says: "It [science] is morally and emotionally neutral. It sets out to describe and understand, not to appraise and assign values. Indeed science is without a scale of values: the only value which it recognizes is that of truth and knowledge."[3] He goes on to say that what man will do with the new facts and control over nature which science gives him is not the concern of science but depends on his scale of values. It is the business of religion to provide an adequate scale of values by which to determine conduct and "to provide emotional or spiritual driving forces to help in getting them realized in practice."

From these testimonies it is apparent that religion has a vital function to perform which science will never destroy. Science seeks for the facts of life; religion its values. Science provides the effective means; religion the valid goals. Science describes relations and processes; religion interprets their meaning for life. Science is concerned with quantitative considerations; religion the qualitative. Science is concerned with immediate causes; religion with ultimate causes and destiny. While it is perfectly evident that man cannot live effectively in disregard of the facts, neither can he live without goals. We live by facts; we live for goals. Both are necessary and their mutual relationship has received succinct statement in the words of a modern religious writer:

Life is not a circle at whose center either science or religion can ever displace the other. It is an ellipse with science and religion as the two foci. Science is the focus today of the entire effort of man as a species to master

[3] *Science and Religion, A Symposium*, p. 18.

the forces of his world. Religion is the focus of the effort of man as an individual to find the meaning and values of his life. The religious man must use science as the most powerful instrument man has devised for adapting means to ends. The scientist must invoke the moods of religion that life may not lose its significance for the world of human creatures in whose behalf he labors.[4]

MUTUAL DEPENDENCE

Different as are the functions of these two expressions of the human spirit, they must take account of one another. Religion must operate in the real world and not a fancied one. Man has labored under many illusions about the nature of his world, and science has been his liberator by revealing the true facts. If religion is to maintain its contact with reality as understood by each generation, it must take account of the established findings of science. Science may not dictate to religion in the latter's own sphere, but it may well serve as one of religion's correctives, and religion will ignore its contributions at its own peril.

Science on the other hand rests on certain assumptions and finds its incentives in certain propositions that are essentially religious in nature. Science is built upon the assumption of the intelligibility or rationality of the world. It believes not only in an objective truth, but also in the unity of all truth into a single system. This assumption is an article of faith about the universe which is not capable of complete demonstration. Undermine faith in the fact and unity of truth and science will crumble at its foundations.

Furthermore, science proceeds on the assumption that the discovery of the facts about life and world will serve to make human life richer and fuller. The research scientist in order to be the best kind of scientist may attain a high degree of disinterestedness in the particular nature of his findings, but back of his striving is the faith that knowledge may be used for the enrichment of life. Divest life of all great and lasting meaning and there would be little motivation left for carrying on the scientific quest. What would it profit mankind to gain full knowledge of the world only in turn to become extinct? Only on the assumption that life has meaning and that knowledge of facts and ability to control natural forces will contribute to the realization of

---

[4] J. W. Nixon, *An Emerging Christian Faith*, p. 120. Harper & Brothers, 1930.

that meaning is science justified in all its effort. The realm of meaning and values and their fulfillment is, however, the province of religion.

Unless the new facts and controls which science puts into men's hands are placed under high ethical controls they will become the means of human disaster rather than the enrichment of life. The coming of the atomic age has multiplied this danger. Civilization is threatened on many sides with catastrophe because man's knowledge has outrun his moral responsibility, and it would appear that only a religion with a high ethical sense at its center, and with a vision of a glorious order of life as a guide, is adequate to safeguard civilization from the destructive possibilities of that new knowledge.

RELATION TO PHILOSOPHY AND THE ARTS

It is conceivable that certain readers of this chapter may bring the charge against it that the functions attributed to religion in this discussion are in fact problems of philosophy and that philosophy is not receiving its due recognition. The writer has no desire to slight philosophy for without its co-operation religion could not render an adequate service to any age. Problems of meaning, value, destiny and ultimate reality are in truth philosophic problems. They do not exhaust philosophy's concerns, but they are important items on the list. Religion must depend upon philosophy to help it find the best answers to its basic questions about life. A philosophy is one of religion's essential aspects. Religion, however, is more extensive than its philosophy for it must press beyond theory to actual effort to realize its ends and goals in living experience. Religion includes a way of life as well as a philosophy of life; it involves techniques as well as ends, activities as well as interpretations. Religion has the larger and more inclusive task, but in carrying out its task in the interpretative aspects it must welcome the contribution of philosophy, as on the side of its active program it must also welcome the contributions of the fine and practical arts and of the applied sciences.

In conclusion it may be said that science, the great enemy of superstition, is not the enemy of intelligent religion and will not displace it. Religion is not established by science, but modern scientific revelations about the structure of the universe by no means exclude, nor are they unfavorable to, a spiritual interpretation of life. Few eminent scientists today are materialists in their own philosophy. It would seem that the day has come for the representatives of these two great interests to lay aside hostilities and to join hands in work together for the greatest era of material plenty and spiritual quality that the world has ever known.

CHAPTER IV

Living by Faith

ACCORDING to the dictionary the term "faith" has a number of different uses, and as one surveys these he is made to realize that it is frequently used very loosely. For religion it is an absolutely necessary concept, however, and when used in critical discussion, it should be given a very definite meaning acceptable to the participants in the discussion. Its use in this discourse will be in accord with this definition: faith is belief expressed in appropriate action. Considered in this way, it has its roots in intellectual conviction, but it goes beyond the intellectual into moral affirmation. Its test is action, not merely assent. Faith means taking the risks involved in translating belief into actual conduct. One may believe, for instance, that an automobile is safe for travel at high speed. That belief is translated into faith when one enters the car and actually travels in it at high speed.

FAITH AND KNOWLEDGE

Faith has its basis in knowledge but is not restricted to knowledge for its foundation. Knowledge is another term subject to wide variation and usage. In this discussion knowledge will be taken to mean "certified information," that is, information that has been tested for truth. The more that knowledge enters into the structure of one's faith, the more certain that faith will be, and the less the risk involved in taking the action determined by the faith. But faith cannot be limited to matters of which we have certain knowledge for two reasons. In the first place, our capacity for knowledge is too limited for us to have complete information about everything in which we must place our trust. In the second place, the existing knowledge about many vital matters in life is very partial and decidedly incomplete. So much is this true that if we attempted to live on the basis of knowledge alone, acting only when the action was fully justified by certified facts, we would not be able to live at all, so limited would be the range of possibilities.

Most of our actions are determined on the basis of probabilities rather than thorough-going information. We permit ourselves to relax at night into untroubled sleep, not because we know for a certainty that we shall awake in the morning but on the basis of a high statistical probability. If we insisted upon absolute assurance that the house would not burn down over our heads, or that we would not be overcome with a heart attack, or that no other calamity would befall while sleeping, we would never be able to sleep. When we trust our lives to a bus or an automobile and travel at the rate of fifty or sixty miles an hour on a highway, we cannot know that accident will not overtake us. When we travel in this way we exercise faith in the vehicle, faith in the driver, faith in the road, faith in other drivers on the road, and faith in many other factors which affect the situation, and it is not possible to have full knowledge about all these factors.

The more serious ventures in life always involve a large measure of probability. In choosing a life work one should bring to bear upon the decision all the knowledge possible concerning one's likes and dislikes, aptitudes, skills, and the needs of society for various kinds of service. But the factors to be considered are so numerous that it is impossible for one to determine beforehand the exact degree of success he will attain in a particular vocation. The best he can hope for is an indication of probability as to the degree of his success in a particular field, and upon such he must be willing to act if he selects for himself his life work.

In entering marriage it is highly important that two people should bring to their decision all the knowledge possible concerning each other. It is not enough to know that one is fascinated by the other's beauty and manner or that one feels proud when enjoying the association of one who is acknowledged as handsome. It is necessary to know how large a degree of real community of interest exists between the two personalities. It is necessary to know each other's likes and dislikes; it is important to know something of the heritage which each one brings to the new union. There are many things that it is important to know, but inasmuch as it is impossible for one person to know completely the composition of another's personality especially before they have lived together in intimate relations, there can be no absolute assurance beforehand that any marriage will be crowned with complete success. In this supremely important decision young people must be content with action which finds its best basis in a high degree of probability. In these important decisions faith should be based on the fullest knowledge obtainable but it cannot be restricted to the limits of one's knowledge. In the very nature of the case faith must go beyond the limits which knowledge alone would ordain. Edwin E. Aubrey expresses this necessity in an adaptation of the old saying that a friend is one who knows all about you and still believes in you, to wit, "Religious faith is found at its best in the man who finds out all he can about his world and still believes in it."

RELIGIOUS VERSUS NON-RELIGIOUS FAITH

From the illustrations already given it should be apparent that without faith it is impossible to live at all. Every conscious act, every venture in life is an adventure of faith. In everything we do we commit ourselves to the truth of certain propositions, consciously or unconsciously. In the light of this fact the question which men have to decide is not whether or not they will live by faith, but by what kind of faith will they live. Applied to religion, the irreligious person lives by his faith as surely as the man of religious conviction; the difference lies in the nature of their respective faiths. It is utterly untrue to say that one lives by knowledge, and the other by faith, and likewise false to say that one lives by science and the other by tradition. One person has committed himself to one set of probabilities, the other to another. One lives by non-religious faith, the other by religious faith, and which is the better faith is to be determined by which set of beliefs can command the more convincing and fuller evidence in its support. In neither case will it be possible to offer complete demonstration of the truth or falsity of the position. Man must act on the basis of his judgment as to which position is supported by the greater weight of evidence. Having

made his decision and translated it into appropriate action he lives by
faith.

THE NATURE OF CHRISTIAN FAITH

The great affirmations of religion which become the basis of religious
living represent probabilities rather than fully demonstrated conclusions.
This does not mean that they are not supported by knowledge, but is
to assert that the extent of our present knowledge is not in itself sufficient to establish fully the truth of the conviction. One may establish
the fact of God's existence by definition, that is, by defining God in
terms of that which surely exists beyond doubt. This Professor H. N.
Wieman does. In the introduction to his work, *Religious Experience
and Scientific Method,* he lays down the principle upon which he builds
his whole system of thought:

Whatever else the word God may mean, it is a term used to designate
that Something upon which human life is most dependent for its security,
welfare and increasing abundance. That there is such a Something cannot
be doubted. The mere fact that human life happens, and continues to happen, proves that this Something, however unknown, does certainly exist.

If, as is done here, you define God in terms of that which is known to
exist, obviously you cannot deny his existence. But the minute you turn
from the general concept to a particular description of the nature of
this reality you leave the realm of absolute certainty and enter the realm
of probability. Any description of God which man may perfect will be
subject to question at various points. When religion bases its faith upon
the existence of God of a particular nature, its foundation rests in a
speculation, and the actions which ensue are determined in the light of
a probability and not a certainty. This is true of all the fundamental
convictions which comprise a great religious system. The current Christian convictions are of this nature. Christianity affirms that the Bible
gives us a trustworthy revelation of God and of his will and purposes
for the world. There is no absolute proof that this is true. The same
can be said concerning the beliefs that Jesus is the Son of God and the
Saviour of men, that through prayer men may enter into direct communion with the Deity, that sin is always brought to judgment, that
forgiveness and moral redemption are available to those who meet the

terms, that personal immortality is a real possibility, and that the church is an agency through which divine grace is mediated to men. Christianity affirms the truth of these propositions despite the fact that they cannot be demonstrated completely, and it calls upon men to act upon these propositions as though they were most assuredly true. The person who accepts the challenge is a man of Christian faith; the person who rejects the challenge is a person of non-Christian faith. Although the latter may not adhere to the tenets of any particular system, the beliefs which determine his behavior belong just as surely to the realm of the unproven as do these religious convictions. When he acts upon them he lives by faith. The only rational procedure is to weigh the evidence and to act in accordance with those propositions which are most convincing to your judgment as expressive of the truth.

It would be a mistake, however, to assume that man arrives at his beliefs or determines his highest loyalties through logical processes primarily. Reason may be accorded the privilege of serving as final arbiter between conflicting claims, but it is seldom the means of discovering our foremost loyalties. The higher loyalties of life tend rather to discover us and claim us for themselves by their overpowering effect on our affections. We do not create them but rather the creative impulses in us are awakened by them. They do not depend upon us so much as we depend upon them to bring completion to our lives. This yielding of life, frequently called surrender, to some splendid vision, great cause, or transcendent truth which claims us for itself is of the very essence of religious experience. "Whenever anybody thus finds any goodness, truth, or beauty," says Harry Emerson Fosdick, "concerning which he feels not that it should give itself to him, but that he should give himself to it and be its loyal servant, that man has entered into an authentic religious experience."[1] Dean Robert Russell Wicks declares that a person outgrows a childish stage in religion when he finds some undertaking or cause of which he can say, "I belong to that," and, he adds, "The more significant the enterprise, the happier a man is in belonging to it with all his heart and soul."

Seldom if ever do we put ourselves in the way of such an experience through pure logical processes of thought, but rather by exposing our-

---

[1] *As I See Religion*, p. 11. Harper & Brothers.

selves to the various claims that life may make upon a person until that which we recognize as of supreme worth lays hold upon us. We invite such experience when we extend the boundaries of our knowledge and develop our appreciation of higher values as these have been determined in the experience of the race. When the supreme claim asserts itself we are called up to make the most important decision of life. In that connection. W. A. Visser 't Hooft points out that when we see this moment in perspective we discover a strange thing. "We find that the most active moment of life was also the most passive. For we could only choose because we were being chosen. We could only accept because we were being accepted. We found power to decide because we were being overpowered."[2]

To claims for our loyalty and devotion, whether they be great or small, whether they be high or low, reason may justly be applied as a test and that which is contrary to reason becomes suspect at once. When, however, reason does not contradict but lends support, commitment is justified. The consecrations which result from the claim of a high ideal, however, are always ventures of faith, the translation of convictions into appropriate action. As the very essence of religion is the commitment of life to certain truths and ideals as worthy of the highest devotion, faith is the core of religion.

Throughout the remainder of this book, attention will be directed to considerations which affect the balance both for and against the acceptance of current religious beliefs as veritably true. Is an adequate basis for faith provided in our inherited religious beliefs? We shall seek an answer to this question in relation to the specific affirmations which constitute the Christian heritage.

[2] *None Other Gods*, p. 13. Harper & Brothers.

CHAPTER V

Is the Bible the Word of God?

MAN has been a resident upon the earth for hundreds of thousands of years according to the conclusions of scientists, but the historical record of his progress reaches back only six thousand years. It is significant that the Bible was in process of production for a thousand years or during one-sixth of the time of historic record. This thousand years occurred between the approximate dates of 850 B.C. and 150 A.D., a period in which great advances were registered in the development of civilization. The Bible which is the greatest literary product of this age represents a collection of works of diverse character produced in a success of changing times and circumstances. Some of the materials incorporated in the Old Testament were in writing much earlier than 850 B.C., but that date marks the beginning of an effort to collect them into organized form. Probably the earliest works in the Old Testament to be completed as we now have them were the writings of the great prophets who preceded the Babylonian exile, beginning with Amos who delivered his oracles about the middle of the eighth century, B.C. The historical books which deal with earlier periods were worked over several times and did not receive their final form until after the exile. The last book of the New Testament to be composed, according to the conclusion of the scholars, was the so-called Second Epistle of Peter and is to be dated about 150 A.D.

As the Bible reflects a succession of changing times, it is likewise distinctly varied in the types and styles of literature which it includes. One can find within its covers myths, legends, allegories, battle songs, hymns, short stories, poetry, law, history, ritual, philosophy, prophecy, proverbs, biographies, letters, and apocalypses or revelations. Despite these diversities there is a unity in the Bible, however, in that it is concerned with the experience of a people marked by a genius for religion in their dealing with God and their efforts to carry out his will and program in the world.

With its two major divisions everyone is familiar, that of the Old Testament which comprises the scriptures of the Jews; and the New Testament, the added scriptures of the Christians. The Old Testament, in turn, may be divided into three divisions known as the Law, the Prophets, and the Writings, respectively. The Law includes the first five books of the Bible, commonly known as the books of Moses and sometimes referred to as the Pentateuch. This is the most important section of the scriptures for orthodox or traditional Judaism. The Prophets include not only the works of the so-called major and minor prophets, beginning with Isaiah and continuing through Malachi, but also certain books commonly regarded as historical works, namely, Joshua, Judges, Samuel and Kings. The Writings represent a rather miscellaneous group of compositions not included in the first two classifications, Job, Psalms, and Proverbs being among the most important of these. The New Testament includes four brief biographies of Jesus Christ, known as the Gospels, an historical work of church history, entitled "The Acts of the Apostles," a collection of letters by the Apostle Paul, other letters by other Christian leaders, and an apocalypse, or book of mystical revelation, entitled, "The Revelation of John."

THEORY OF VERBAL INSPIRATION

The most popular definition of the Bible among Christians declares it to be "the inspired word of God." There is, however, a considerable divergence of opinion as to the meaning of this phrase. In past generations, especially in Protestant circles since the Reformation, the majority view has favored the theory of verbal inspiration, which declares that the truth and accuracy of the very words of the original text were guaranteed by the authority of God. If we follow the most scholarly exponent of this theory of recent years, the late J. G. Machen, this does not mean that the Bible is equally beautiful or equally valuable in all of its parts but that it is equally true in every portion. This scholar refused also to admit any mechanical explanation of the Bible's origin, declaring against the theory that God actually dictated the words in a way that business and professional men dictate letters to their secretaries. He affirms that the writers engaged in study and research, and that they drew upon other writings for information and made use of human authorities. The writers were well aware of what they were doing when they wrote and the meaning of their utterances, although he concedes they may not have appreciated the full meaning and significance of the things they wrote. Although they made use of ordinary sources of information and wrote in normal human styles, the theory of verbal inspiration maintains that these writers were guaranteed by supernatural means from falling into error. "To err is human, and these men did not err," says Professor Machen. "They were always protected in supernatural fashion from the errors which appear in ordinary books." To the same author we are obliged for the following succinct statement of the doctrine of plenary inspiration of Holy scriptures.

I hold that the Biblical writers, after having been prepared for their task by the providential ordering of their entire lives, received, in addition to all that, a blessed and wonderful and supernatural guidance and impulsion by the Spirit of God, so that they were preserved from the errors that appear in other books and thus the resulting book, the Bible, is in all its parts the very Word of God, completely true in what it says regarding matters of fact and completely authoritative in its commands.[1]

According to this view the Bible represents the statement of absolute truth from whatever angle you choose to test it. If the Bible asserts certain things about the physical nature of the universe, then these things are true, irrespective of what scientists may say, for the Bible is guaranteed by God himself. History in the Bible may not be complete, but insofar as there are historical accounts these are in no way in error. The moral judgments expressed in the Bible represent the judgments of God, and, although they may not always be understood by the human mind, their justification is not subject to question. To be sure, allowance must be made at every point for human fallibility in interpretation, but once it is determined exactly what the Bible says about any subject, that statement may be accepted as veritable truth. The ad-

[1] *Christian Faith in the Modern World,* p. 36 f.

vantage of this theory is that it undergirds religious faith with an absolute authority. This, to many minds, is a priceless asset to be maintained at all cost.

To the mind which is open on the question of Biblical authority, certain obstacles loom up large to the acceptance of belief in verbal inspiration. Discrepancies are apparent in the Biblical material. An early illustration of this is found in the two accounts of creation in the first and second chapters of Genesis, respectively. The first account begins with the creation of the world itself and of the heavenly bodies and proceeds to the creation of life, first in the form of vegetation, then successively the creatures that live in the water, the birds of the air, animals, reptiles, wild beasts, and finally as the climax of the process, man, both male and female. In the second account, before there were any plants in the fields or shrubs on the earth, God molded a man out of the dust of the ground. Then he proceeded to plant a garden in which he placed this creature where he caused all manner of plants and trees to grow. The story tells how God molded out of the ground the wild beasts and birds of the air. Finally, in order to provide man with a companion, he took one of his ribs while the man was in a deep sleep and built upon it a woman. Not only are there marked differences in these two accounts in literary style and vocabulary and philosophic conceptions, but the order of events is so different as to make it impossible to reconcile them with one another. If one reads on a few chapters to the story of the deluge, he finds discrepancies within what appears on the surface as a single account of this catastrophe. According to certain verses, Noah took into the ark two of every species of birds, animals, and reptiles, of both the clean and the unclean; but a few verses later, it is stated that of the clean animals, he took seven pairs of each. According to certain verses the rain which brought the flood fell for forty days and nights. According to another statement the waters rose on the earth for one hundred and fifty days. It would be possible to go on and accumulate a large number of such discrepancies within the record. The only defense that advocates of inspiration can offer is that these discrepancies are apparent rather than real. In similar manner it can be shown that although the Bible contains much verified history, it also contains statements which, according to the findings of archeological and historical research, are inaccuracies.

From the standpoint of moral standards, certain things are commanded by God in the early history of Hebrew migrations and settlement in Canaan that are quite contrary to the character of God as he is portrayed later in the record and particularly in the teachings of Jesus. It would be difficult, for instance, to ascribe to the God of Jesus' teaching, who advocated love even for enemies, such a command as is recorded in Judges 21:10, 11 where he ordered the soldiers of Israel to put to the sword the inhabitants of Jabesh-Gilead, along with the women and children. The upholders of the theory of verbal inspiration do not attempt to deny this, but they divide the history of the world into a series of dispensations, in each of which God acted differently with respect to the world of men. So it is not required that there should be any constancy in the mode of God's action in various ages. God was justified in acting one way under the dispensation of the law and in a very different way under the dispensation of grace. To many minds this manner of accounting for the conflicts in moral ideals is at best an example of ingenious rationalization, and is no real solution of the changing moral attitudes which are evident in the Bible. In the face of such difficulties proponents of the theory of verbal inspiration have been fighting a losing battle against advancing knowledge and a more general acquaintance with the contents of the book.

A PROGRESSIVE REVELATION

Christian views of the inspiration of the Bible will be found to cover a wide range. If we may consider the theory of verbal inspiration as representing one pole of thought, the theory of progressive revelation may be considered as the opposite pole. According to this view God reveals himself through the medium of the Bible, but that revelation was fitted and accommodated to the understanding of men in the successive ages during which the Bible was being produced. In the days of the childhood of the race, men were capable of only childish ideas of God and of his will for the world. In an age when folk-lore was the only literature, a revelation recorded in writing would make use of that particular literary form, for there was no other. Such literature is by its very nature limited in its ability to convey the highest concepts of the nature and activity of God. But it is surprising to modern readers how successfully these ancient authors made use of this medium despite its limitations in the teaching of exalted religious conceptions and noble moral ideals. Before there were developed any canons regulating the writing of history it was not to be expected that men writing religious treatises would be free from errors in historical matters, and in writings of a pre-scientific era one should not look for accord with later scientific views of the world. Within the limitations which the times imposed upon the understanding of men, God revealed himself to the extent of their ability to apprehend. Even in matters religious they were given to error, therefore, because of their inability to receive the full truth. As time went on and civilization developed, and as men's understanding grew, God was able to reveal himself in fuller and truer fashion.

One may think of this relationship as that of a choral director endeavoring to reveal his knowledge of music to a community. Provide him with a chorus of people without musical training or experience and he would have to begin teaching them the simplest elements of choral singing. It would require years of development, leading the group on step by step through simple melodies to complex harmonies before he could reveal through such a medium his own understanding and appreciation of great choral music. At each step he is limited in what he can accomplish by the ability of the group to receive and appropriate. Even so in the times when Biblical literature began, God could reveal only the simplest elements of faith and morals to people not far removed from savagery. They were capable of conceiving of God only as one much like themselves, but more powerful and mysterious. It is possible to trace step by step in the writings of the Old Testament the progress of a people with a genius for religion in developing the noblest conception of God and the highest standard of moral action known to the ancient world. In the New Testament this process reaches its culmination in the person, character, and teachings of Jesus Christ.

The authors of the books of the Bible were men of their own times whose minds were illuminated sufficiently to perceive the next step in the process in a growing understanding of God and of his will for men. The essence of inspiration is this experience of illumination through which one perceives clearly truth not before fully grasped. Inspiration so understood, however, does not guarantee one against error in other matters beyond the limit of the new insight. The human qualities and limitations of the authors of the Bible are apparent at every turn, but through their experiences the revelation of God developed through its successive stages. What from the human standpoint is an insight, from the divine standpoint is a revelation. Inspiration results whenever men, who seek to know, have their minds enlightened through the activity of God who seeks to reveal himself. Professor George Walter Fiske summarizes this view of the Bible as follows:

The Bible is a record of the progressive revelation of God to men and a history of the growth of religion from crude early forms up to its full purity and authority in Jesus Christ.[2]

The view of the Bible as a progressive revelation frees it from the charges that may be leveled against it when the theory of verbal inspiration is applied. Misconceptions and errors in the early portion of the work are to be expected as is their elimination in the later portion of the work. The standards which should prevail and by which all should be judged are the highest to be found within the covers of the book.

Although this theory meets the criticism brought against the theory of verbal inspiration, it should also be observed that it forfeits the one great advantage which attached to that theory, namely, absolute authority. It would be unfair to say that it forfeits all the authority of the Bible, for there is always authority even in a partial revelation just as there is authority in all knowledge concerning some subject of inquiry, although neither the revelation nor the knowledge may represent the last word to be spoken in these regards. Just as scientific knowledge is authoritative until a higher knowledge has emerged, so a divine revelation is authoritative until it has been superseded by a higher one. But so long as there is open the possibility of going beyond present attainments or understanding, the existing conceptions cannot be regarded as absolute. Many people fear the surrender of absolute authority for it seems to them like losing their anchor. Others, however, are not frightened by the prospect of sailing the high seas so long as they have a reasonably accurate chart and compass even though these may not be absolutely free from error.

Those who accept the theory of progressive revelation must sooner

[2] *The Changing Family,* p. 256 f.

or later face the question as to whether or not God's revelation was completed in the Bible. Presumably if the increasing ability of men to understand resulted in successively higher revelations, may we not expect that process to continue in the future as it has in the past? For Christians this involves the question of the finality of the revelation found in Christ. There are those who hold the progressive view who maintain that in Christ was revealed all of God that can ever be revealed through a human person. There are others, however, who would assert that whereas the revelation of Christ is final in the sense that it will not be overthrown, it may in the future be added to and expanded, but the new additions will represent a further development or unfolding of truths already inherent in his revelation. Jesus stands as the highest expression up to this time of a revelation which is continually progressive and inexhaustible. On this basis it is conceivable that other writings that have the ability to inspire men may come to be regarded as scripture, and may form a new section of the sacred canon, even as the New Testament was added to the Old.

NEO-ORTHODOX VIEW

In a day when a mode of thought, generally known as neo-orthodoxy in this country, has come to prevail generally in Protestant circles in Europe, and has gained a large following in America, it should be in order to set forth briefly the attitude of this school toward the Bible. This is not an easy assignment. The words of Karl Barth, the foremost European leader of this movement, are abstruse. As the exposition of Emil Brunner, who is second in importance to Barth in the intellectual leadership of this school of thought, is much clearer, we shall seek to set forth the essence of his view of the matter.

The members of this school reject outright the theory of verbal inspiration, for to them it makes an idol of the Bible. They accept the established conclusions of historical and literary criticism of the Bible, and some of their number have made significant contributions to this discipline. The Bible is a human book, subject to error, and among the many forms of its literature there is recognized a large element of legend and myth. While those of this persuasion readily accept the findings of the newer scientific and historical methods of Biblical study, they adhere firmly to the truths of religion as expressed in the historic creeds of the church, and for this reason are called neo-orthodox. They make much of the claim that their faith is Biblically grounded.

Almost equally unacceptable to them as the theory of verbal inspiration is that of progressive revelation. While they would acknowledge that there is progress of thought in the Bible, they would deny that this is the heart of the matter for reasons that will become apparent in what follows.

According to Emil Brunner the words which constitute the Bible are human words and are not therefore in themselves the Word of God. They may, and often do become, however, the medium through which the Word of God comes to man. The true word is a living word, not something that can be inscribed in a book. The most that the latter can do is to bear witness to the fact and presence of the living word on the part of prophets and apostles who have experienced that word in themselves. The Christ is the living word, but the Christ cannot be identified with the historical Jesus as pictured in the New Testament. He is but a shadow of the real substance. The Gospels are only a testimony of those who confronted the living Christ in their experience. Jesus becomes the Christ only when one is himself confronted by the living word firsthand, and sees Him through the eyes of faith. When that takes place the whole Biblical record is illuminated and becomes the medium through which the true Word is imparted to man. The living word reveals to man that which is absolutely unique, and so is not acquired through the exercise of human reason. It must be imparted to man from without, and being above human reason it must carry its own validation. It must be self-authenticating.

Although the Bible, and more particularly Jesus Christ, becomes the medium which the living word uses to express and manifest itself, it is not itself the Word, but simply a human witness or attestation to the presence of the Word and the possibility of its reception by others who open their minds and hearts to its coming. As Brunner says:

> God's word is more than can ever be confined within human language, but it does not come to us a part from human words.[3]

True preaching is that which is doctrinally correct, and its power as a

---

[3] *Reason and Revelation*, p. 151.

witness depends on the degree of that correctness, but not exclusively upon that.

> That which can be definitely and theologically formulated of the message of the Apostles and the other Biblical witnesses forms the basis on which their word can become the Word of God.[4]

Yet he adds:

> I do not believe in Jesus Christ because an Apostle tells me He is the Son of God, which would mean that my belief in Jesus Christ was based on my belief in an Apostle; but I believe in Jesus Christ because God Himself has convinced me that He is the Christ, just as He convinced the Apostle.[5]

There are a number of difficulties in accepting this position, but one of the most critical is that of finding a criterion for judging between true and false interpretations of the word. Since the experience of receiving the living word is highly subjective, it does not readily lend itself to any objective judgment in determining false from true interpretations of the scriptures. A serious problem ensues in safeguarding the revelation from the vagaries of human interpretation which claim immediate divine authority.

MIRACLES

Young people who have acquired something of the scientific temper of this age find a difficulty in the miracles of the Bible for the dictum of science seems to be that miracles do not happen. What then shall we do with the "disturbing miracles"? For those who accept the theory of verbal inspiration of the Bible, there seems to be no alternative to the acceptance of these records as relating to facts which occurred exactly as they are reported. Those that cannot be accounted for in terms of natural forces must be accepted as expressions of supernatural activity, which on occasion may intervene in or set aside the natural order.

Those who find the developmental theory of Biblical inspiration preferable will probably make other interpretations of these events. They recognize that the term "miracle" has had different meanings for differ-

---

[4] *Ibid.*, p. 151.
[5] *Ibid.*, p. 169.

ent ages and people. For our purpose it will be sufficient to consider two of these meanings. According to one view, a miracle refers to an intervention into the natural order on the part of some supernatural power. The other view holds that a miracle is an unusual event, the explanation of which exceeds man's present understanding. It is rather assumed, according to this second view, that such events are not contrary to the natural law but will be found to be quite in accord with it when the full explanation becomes possible. Many of the cures accredited to Jesus are today being duplicated through the use of psychotherapy. Cases with very startling symptoms have been completely cured through the ministrations of an understanding psychologist in the field of mental hygiene without resort to medicines or treatments of any other kind. By invoking a wholesome and healthful attitude of mind in the patient, fears were replaced by confidence, a sense of futility gave way to faith in the essential goodness of life, symptoms cleared up, and cures of an amazing nature have been effected. Such incidents are not regarded as miracles today because man knows too much about the processes by which they are achieved. It is not necessary, therefore, to regard the cures effected by Jesus as in any sense a violation of natural laws, and most liberal scholars are ready to concede that through his ability to inspire new attitudes toward life in the minds of men, he was able to effect many remarkable cures. Such an explanation will not account, however, for many of the Biblical miracles, and particularly those that are called nature miracles. Some of these latter may have been natural phenomena, such as the plagues that were inflicted on the people in Egypt at the time when Moses was seeking to lead the Israelites out of bondage, and the drying of the bed of the Red Sea by a strong east wind which blew the water back, allowing the people to cross on dry land. There is also the suggestion in connection with the crossing of the Jordan by these tribes that a landslide had served to dam the river temporarily, cutting off its flow for sufficient time to allow the people to cross over. These fortunate natural phenomena were interpreted as direct manifestations of divine power for the particular benefit of the Children of Israel. But the distinction which modern man makes between natural events and supernatural occurrences was foreign to the ancient's mode of thought. Gaius Glenn Atkins has given splendid expression to this fact:

The persuasion of Jahweh's absolute dominion over any force or event seams Hebrew devotion. Anything becomes possible for him and his servants; iron may float, rivers be parted, a drenched altar so kindled that the very stones are burnt. Given a people who have no scientific sense of natural law, a world in which there is no law at all but Jahweh's will and such things are, for the narrator, as natural as anything else. This is the key to wonder narratives of early Hebrew history.[6]

Miracles were no problem for the men of Bible times and when we understand that fact, they become less a problem for modern minds, because we realize that had the explanation of these events been framed by men of scientific training, they would have been expressed differently.

In pre-scientific eras a favorite method of testifying to the greatness of a person whose accomplishments were astonishing to his own and succeeding generations was the medium of a miracle tradition. Miracle stories grew up spontaneously about such figures. They may have had little basis in fact but were not deliberate falsifications. They became true expressions of society's estimate of a great person's power stated in ways that were normal to the times. A miracle tradition gathered about an ancient worthy was a reliable witness to the fact that he made an unusual impression on the life of his time.

Even today many people justify the acceptance of the more difficult miracles associated with Jesus on the grounds that one of such marvelous character, who enjoyed so vital a union with God as characterized his life, would be capable through perfectly natural means of accomplishments beyond the power of ordinary men. In such a case it is noteworthy that the miracles serve not as arguments for supporting faith in Jesus as the Son of God, but the belief in Jesus as the Son of God justified on moral and spiritual grounds supports the acceptance of the miracles as facts.

Irrespective of the final judgment upon particular miracles in the Bible, it should be noted that the idea of the miraculous represents an essential principle in religion. This is not to require that some events must occur in contravention of the natural order, but is to assert that religion is grounded in the faith that neither God nor men are prison-

---

[6] Atkins and Braden, *The Procession of the Gods*, p. 393.

ers within an impersonal order which permits no freedom of action or really creative achievement. In a world where creative action is possible things surprising to men will continue to happen. In the realm of practical science, recent decades have seen the appearance of a series of modern miracles. Things which seemed utterly impossible to previous generations have come to be taken for granted by this generation. The fact that a few men can explain such phenomena as the automobile, the airplane, the radio, and the wireless telephone makes these things no less wonderful to the mass of men and their emergence has been nothing if not surprising. What is possible in the realm of practical science is also true in the operation of religious and moral forces. The recognition of this fact has called forth from Harry Emerson Fosdick the following significant declaration:

A miracle is God's use of his own law-abiding powers to work out in ways surprising to us his will for our lives and for the world. Unless the whole Christian Gospel is false, miracles in that sense are happening all the time. If I had not experienced them and seen them I should not be a Christian at all.[7]

THE BIBLE'S FUTURE

What about the future of the Bible in the experience of men? The present is obviously a time in which the Bible is being neglected as compared with the devotion given it by previous generations. Are we to infer from this that the Bible is to drop out as one of the major forces determining the nature of the new culture? It can be answered with assurance that this will be true only if the Christian religion itself ceases to be a powerful force within that culture. The Christian religion finds its center in devotion to Jesus Christ and the truth of God which he has made plain. Remove Jesus Christ from this religious system and it would completely collapse. Virtually man's whole knowledge of Jesus Christ is contained within the New Testament, and the Old Testament is the record of what preceded and led up to his coming. It is inconceivable, therefore, that the Christian religion can continue to function without constant reference to the Bible as the Book of Jesus Christ. In certain ages it may fall into comparative obscurity as men

[7] *The Modern Use of the Bible.* Chapter V, p. 162.

live on the momentum of faith generated by a previous generation, but a succeeding age will just as assuredly go back to the original sources for fresh insight and inspiration, and so stimulate great revivals of interest in the message of the book. The Bible has been a lamp unto men's feet and a light unto their pathway, and so it will continue to be unless Christian culture disintegrates. No other book is comparable to it in its effects in shaping the life of men and nations in their endeavors to express the divine will for life. As God has spoken to men in the past through the pages of this book, and will continue to reach their hearts and minds through this medium in the future, it may most fittingly be called The Word of God.

CHAPTER VI

How Shall We Think of God?

FAITH in God is the basic article of religious faith. In the thinking of men, however, there have been many gods who have been variously represented and approached by various modes. It is evident that if religion is going to function, man must have a working idea of the nature of God which will determine the kind of adjustments which he will strive to make to the divine order of life. In endeavoring to build up a working concept of God, one must proceed very carefully as there are many pitfalls.

It is important, in the first place, to distinguish between the fact of God and any particular idea of God. God is greater than man's comprehension of him, which means that man's best ideas will be only approximations of the truth. If God did not exceed man's comprehension he would not be God, for man is as great as that which he can fully understand. If he could fully understand the nature and ways of God, he would be the equal of God. Because this is surely not the case, man must be content to deal with symbols which are inadequate to express the full nature of the reality. Oftentimes, however, men fail to differentiate between the symbol and the reality for which it is an imperfect representation. The result is, if their customary symbol is shown to be quite inadequate and impossible of intelligent acceptance, they conclude that there is no God and begin to regard themselves as atheists. All that they really have a right to conclude is that the idea of God which they have entertained is in need of revision. Thoroughgoing atheism is rather rare and exceedingly difficult to maintain, for as Professor Walter M. Horton affirms, complete atheism means that there is nothing in life worth living for. The student, therefore, who finds that the ideas of God which he formulated in his childhood are no longer tenable has not thereby become an atheist. He may be floundering on a sea of uncertainty, and may greatly need some new ideas about the nature of the object of supreme devotion; but he is not justified in denying the existence of God simply because one idea of God is no longer useful.

In the effort to construct a working concept of God, it is well to recognize from the start that except for rare creative geniuses we cannot think beyond the elements of our own experience. With the aid of the imagination we can effect new organizations or patterns of the elements of experience so as to imagine ourselves in situations where we have never actually been or can visualize objects which we have never laid eyes upon, but the only thing new about these products of imagination is a new combination of and not an extension of actual experience. God is greater than our experience of him, but our thought of him will be limited by the extent of our experience in life. The problem becomes that of selecting out of the total body of human experiences, those elements which will best serve as symbols to indicate the nature of that reality which we call God. If God represents that force or object in life which is most worthy of man's supreme devotion, is it not logical to think of him in terms of the highest that we know in the realm of human experience? The highest that we know is lower than the reality of God, but it represents our nearest approach to what God in himself is. The highest that we know, in other words, will not serve as a fully adequate symbol, but any other symbol would be less adequate.

The question now to be asked, if the above logic is valid, is, "What constitutes the highest we know in the realm of human experience?" Judging the highest by that upon which we place the greatest value, we may say with some confidence that persons represent the high point of creation and the object of greatest value. It is true that men frequently subordinate personal values to economic or political ends, but when the issue is clear between the loss of property or the loss of personal life, property will be sacrificed before persons. Economic, political, and social systems eventually are judged by their contribution to the enrichment of the life of people. So far as we are able to see, the evolutionary process has reached its highest development in man, and by personality we mean those qualities of life which differentiate humans from lower forms.

GOD AS PERSON

Because personality represents the highest thing we know in human experience, we are justified in thinking of God in terms of personal qualities. But it is necessary to define carefully what is meant when one thinks of God in personal terms. Does it mean, for instance, that we ascribe to God a physical body like unto a human form? This is very often done and men visualize God as a heavenly king seated on a magnificent golden throne away off somewhere in the skies. Sometimes he is pictured as a judge with long hair and flowing white beard who pores over the record in the book of life. In some homes where parental discipline needs bolstering, God is represented as a super-policeman, spying out the wickedness of men that he may inflict punishment upon them in which practice he takes great delight. It requires little serious thought to realize that such childish conceptions are not compatible with man's present knowledge of the nature of the universe. The trouble arises, however, from man's disposition to attach too much importance to the body as an aspect of personality. To be sure, so far as our present experience goes, man must have a body to serve as an instrument of his larger personality, but that which makes man a person is not his physical equipment. As man requires a body through which to function, it may also be that God functions through the physical universe but the functions are so different that it becomes impossible to ascribe to God a physical nature in any way resembling man's. That which distinguishes man, however, from lower forms of life and so constitutes him a person is not a body. We must look deeper for the essential elements of personality.

The clearest mark of personality is intelligence. Animals, to be sure, have a degree of this, but between a normal man and the highest of the lower animals, there is a vast difference in this respect. Man has powers of intelligence far beyond that of any other creature. Together with intelligence we must take note of a person's ability to experience deep feeling. Again we recognize that all creatures with a nervous system are capable of some degree of feeling, but between the feelings of animals and the conscious love or hatred, indignation or appreciation of man there is a difference so great as to be virtually qualitative. Another certain mark of personality is the ability to conceive and execute a purpose. A person is one who can visualize desirable ends and goals and direct himself toward the fulfillment of those ends in the future. As he can project himself thus in the future, he can also reach back through memory and recover the past. Involved in all of this and a very important element in it is self-consciousness, or the ability of a person to distinguish between that which is himself and that which is not himself. Animals probably have little ability to distinguish between themselves and their environment. This attainment is one of the marks of personality. Another trait unique among persons is the ability to make moral distinctions, to distinguish between right and wrong, and to suffer the pangs of a guilty conscience when the right is denied in favor of the wrong. When men ascribe personality to God they mean, therefore, that there are elements in his nature which correspond to self-consciousness, intelligence, purpose, feeling, appreciation, memory and moral judgment in man. These qualities in their highest degree must characterize God, or some like them which exceed human understanding and for which man has no adequate symbols. To think of God as personal is to conceive of him in the terms of the highest that we know. It must be emphasized in ascribing such qualities to God, however, that one must not picture them with their usual human limitations.

To ascribe personality to God is not to deny that he may function in impersonal ways in large areas of life. This is true of the human organism, although a person may direct his life in large measure on the basis of conscious likes or dislikes, or in accord with an intelligently conceived purpose. It is none the less very much to his advantage that much of his physical organism operates automatically and unconsciously and when functioning properly requires no attention on his part. If the laws of the physical universe in some way describe the operations of God within nature, then much of God's activity proceeds on the impersonal basis. That which is personal may find it advantageous to function through impersonal sequences. To conceive of God wholly in impersonal terms, however, would be quite unsatisfactory, for this would seem to make impossible a real commerce between man and

God as the personal cannot enter into a real communion with the impersonal.

In this connection it is of interest to take note of the position of neo-orthodoxy, a school of thought to which reference was made in the preceding chapter. Adherents of this position minimize the importance of divine immanence, that is, God manifest in creation and in the government of nature as a source of significant revelation. God's presence in nature is not denied, but natural revelation is not a source of saving faith. Instead the transcendence of God is greatly emphasized, even to the point of denying any likeness between God and man. "For my thoughts are not your thoughts, neither are your ways my ways, says the Lord." (Isaiah 55:8.) God is declared to be the "Wholly Other," signifying a complete qualitative difference between man and God. Paul Tillich speaks of "the measureless distance between the infinite and the finite." Here is a gulf which cannot be bridged from the side of man. God can be known only through an act of self-revelation in which he condescends to make himself known to man. The experience is in the nature of a direct encounter, usually described as "I-Thou." To speak of this as an "I-It" relationship would horrify the exponents of this position. God is Person in an absolute sense. But it should be remembered that all we know of Person has been learned from contact with human persons. Representatives of this school of thought often refer to God as Sovereign, Creator, Reconciler, Redeemer and Lord when wishing to designate various divine functions, and they freely ascribe to him such attributes as love, grace, mercy and freedom. It may be remarked that every one of these terms takes its meaning from our experience with other human persons. While it is important to emphasize the range of difference between the divine and human person, if we were forbidden to think of God in the likeness of man, we could have no knowledge of him whatsoever.

OBSTACLES TO BELIEF IN GOD

It is not an easy thing to maintain a constant faith in the existence of God as one with whom man may enter into personal relations. Serious obstacles to such belief arise in the experience of every thinking person. If men were content to define God as that object or force in life most worthy of man's supreme devotion, then it could be maintained that it would be impossible to deny the existence of God inasmuch as there must be something in life which represents the highest object to which man should devote himself. The problem would then become not to prove the existence of God, but to discover what it is in life that deserves man's highest devotion. On this basis the object most worthy of devotion might not correspond with the basic and sustaining forces of nature. There are philosophers of religion who make the empirical approach who are unwilling to make such an identification. They declare that ultimate reality and God are not one and the same. For the most part, however, religious thinkers have been inclined to insist that the ultimate controlling forces in nature are of such character and quality as to be worthy of man's highest devotion. They identify God, therefore, with the ultimate power in the universe. Out of this assumption serious problems for religious faith arise.

For the practical man the greatest difficulty he has to meet in maintaining his faith in God is the fact of so much suffering and evil in the world of his experience. If God is altogether righteous and in control of the forces of nature, why should there be so great a sum of pain and undeserved suffering in a God-ruled world? This is a problem for which no one has been able to submit a completely satisfying answer. A number of partial explanations of the fact of evil can be advanced, but taken altogether they do not provide the complete answer. It is maintained, for instance, that man brings much suffering upon himself by reason of his own folly when he attempts to disregard the established processes of nature. Electric power is a great boon to mankind, but if man through his carelessness or ignorance comes in contact with a high tension current, the result can be only severe injury or death. Such risks seem to be required in a world of dependable forces. Otherwise this would be a fool's paradise, and a much less desirable world than we now know. Similar evil consequences must be expected from violations of the moral order and justly so. The failure of man to abide by the laws of the moral order, while not the sole cause, is without doubt the principal source of evil in human experience.

Many would willingly concede that God cannot properly be charged with the evil which results from men's moral failures; but, they would say, the real question concerns the suffering of the innocent. How can God be just and permit innocent persons to suffer for wrongs in which they have had no part? If the evils of life were distributed in proportion to guilt, and the goods of life in accordance with righteousness, so that each person would suffer or be blessed in accordance with his own deserts, then one could believe that justice rules the life of the world. But those who advocate a law of exact requital as a test of divine justice are very shortsighted. What would it mean if everyone received just what he deserved in terms of his own conduct, so much goodness so much reward, so much evil so much suffering? Such a law would destroy the nature of society. Society is not a collection of isolated individuals acting independently of one another, but a fabric in which lives are so interwoven that whatever affects one affects all. We suffer together and we rejoice together. The evil of one brings suffering to many, and the good of one will be a source of blessing to many. On any other basis life would scarcely be tolerable. If what one person does should have no effect upon the welfare of another, but only on his own, there would be no place for self-giving love in which one gives himself freely to the good of others. In endeavoring to determine the advisability of a certain line of conduct, the only question to be asked would be, "What will be the effect of this action on me?" With real outgoing love removed from life it would be intolerable. For the development of unselfish and noble character far better that we have a world in which we suffer together, and in which we are blessed together.

Pain, it is noted, has disciplinary value. Pain in the human body serves as a warning of dangers that threaten unless precautions are taken or one's mode of life changed. In the field of human relations disappointment and grief may reveal the presence of injustice and maladjustment in the social order and supply the incentive to set things right and make a greater happiness available to all. When pain and suffering serve as the stimuli to personal or social progress they become the instruments of a developing good.

It is also maintained that the development of moral stamina requires the possibility of exercising real choices between good and evil. If men are not to be mere automata in the moral realm, they must struggle against real temptations in order to develop moral fiber. Moral growth takes place only when one chooses the good in preference to the evil. Evil as a possibility must be real, therefore, in a moral order. The function of religion at this point is not so much to explain evil as to furnish man a means of dealing with it and overcoming it. But when all the things are said that can be said in explanation of the fact of evil in life, the conviction lingers that the evil of life has not been sufficiently explained; and as long as this conviction remains it makes difficult faith in a God who is at once the force underlying the operations of nature and the object worthy of man's supreme devotion.

Another obstacle to belief is the fact that the existence of a God with whom men may enter personal relationships has not been sufficiently demonstrated. Many persons are themselves convinced of the existence of such a God on the basis of their own personal experiences, but when another examines their claims, he always finds it possible to offer other possible explanations of the particular experiences than those presented by the man of faith. As long as alternative explanations are possible no one can claim scientific demonstration of the supposed fact. Similarly it may be argued that science in all its researches has not revealed the existence of a God which would satisfy religious needs. On the assumptions of materialism science in the past has achieved a degree of progress which is embarrassing to philosophers of religion.

It is also necessary for thinking people to face the argument developed by certain schools of psychology that man's faith in God is simply a product of wishful thinking. As man becomes aware of his insecurity and insufficiency in a universe which exceeds his comprehension, he feels the need of a superior power in which he can put his trust even as children are aware of the need for their parents. Because men desire such an object of faith they proceed to project it into their universe when as a matter of fact there is no real justification for this belief beyond their own wish to have it so. It should be noted, however, that personal desires have no bearing on the truth either positively or negatively. They are simply irrelevant. One may point out that many things that men once wished might be true, but at the time were considered to be impossible, have proven in a later time to be possible. The desire may have served as a stimulus to try out or examine new possibilities which led to a large understanding of the truth; but wishes in themselves are useless as criteria of judgment as to what is true, or not true.

It must be admitted that there is force in each one of these positions and that it is not easy to overcome these obstacles. Belief in God seems destined to remain a matter of faith, as faith has been defined in this work, that is, a rational conviction incapable of complete demonstration. All one can hope to determine for the present at least is on which side of the question rests the greater weight of argument.

In ancient times one of the strongest reasons men could advance for belief in the activity of God in the world was the evidence of supernatural activity all about them. When they experienced striking phenomena for which they could not give an adequate account, they ascribed these things to the direct activity of their gods. In pre-scientific times this was a normal mode of thinking and so many things happened beyond man's understanding that there was no scarcity of happenings which pointed to the working of supernatural forces. Miracles, wonders, and strange phenomena of nature were the clearest proofs of the existence of a divine order. In this regard the thinking of intelligent men has undergone a radical change with the development of scientific views of the universe. Many of the old marvels have ceased to be marvels as men have come to understand their causes. Man with his present knowledge is capable of producing greater wonders than those attributed to the old gods and accepted as evidences of their right to homage. The miraculous in the sense of the interruption or contravention of natural processes has become more of an obstacle than a help to man's thought about God. On the other hand, the very fact of an ordered universe has become one of the principal foundations for man's faith in the existence of God.

Order is the product of intelligence. Whenever we read a printed page that has sense and meaning it is because the thoughts put down there have been developed logically in the mind of their author, and the printer has translated them into an ordered arrangement of type which makes possible the dissemination of the ideas. Both the work of the author and the work of the printer is an application of intelligence, and order is the result. Wherever you find an organization which functions with a minimum of friction and a high degree of efficiency, you have an ordered process which is the product of intelligence of one mind or of many. The mechanical achievements of our modern day are further examples of careful organization of forces sometimes in relationships which require great precision. These manifestations of order are also the products of intelligence. Wherever we find order we are justified in assuming that intelligence has been at work. If we find the universe is an ordered universe in all of its phases, with an order that has not been imposed upon it by human intelligence, then it must be the product of some vastly superior intelligence, or God. The fact of universal order is a far more significant argument for the existence of God than apparent evidences of disorder, or capricious action, or the interruption of natural processes could ever be.

Closely related to the argument from the fact of an ordered universe is that which perceives the evolutionary process as a directed process toward the fulfillment of a high purpose. The development of the human species seems not to be adequately accounted for on the basis of chance or by the theory of natural selection taken by itself alone. There seem to be only two alternative explanations of the fact observable in organic evolution of a progress in nature from low forms of life to the highly complex form, the human species. One explanation is the secular one which insists that man is the product of a blind process "which does not know what it is producing, which does not know the difference between good and evil, beauty and ugliness, persons and things." The other possible explanation is that the process has been subject to intelligent direction and represents the working out of a purpose. Science is not yet in a position to affirm or deny the truth of either of these explanations. It is noteworthy, however, that a great many scientific men prefer to believe that the evolutionary process is the expression of intelligent purpose. Although science does not establish this, in its present state it leaves the door wide open for the religious interpretation and many notable men of science accept it as preferable to the secular interpretation. The word of the great naturalist, J. Arthur Thomson, is worthy of attention at this point, as he summarizes his own conclusion on this question:

When we consider the persistent way in which advance in Nature has been secured throughout hundreds of millions of years, the apparent conspiring of conditions that facilitate the advance, the way in which broad foundations are laid that make further advances possible, the gradually increasing dominance of "mind" in the higher reaches of life, and the illumination of the whole process when we see it in the light of Man, who is at his best a not unworthy climax, there is a cumulative suggestion of purpose.

But purpose cannot reside in the System of Nature; it must be referred to an Author.[1]

Just as order in nature leads us to presuppose the operation of intelligence, so evidences of purpose in the evolutionary process imply the presence of a Mind in which the purpose is conceived. As there are evidences of purposive activity in nature, man is justified in believing in God as the author of nature's ends and goals.

Looking at the same facts from a somewhat different angle, it may be argued that the existence of persons presupposes creative forces in nature, capable of producing creatures with personal qualities. On the assumption that a stream cannot rise higher than its source, or that every effect must have an equal and adequate cause, there is that in nature which is of a higher order than human personality for it would appear that the forces which have brought persons into existence have not exhausted themselves but are making for the development of a higher order of men than has yet been achieved. It is difficult to see how the impersonal could produce the personal, or how lower forms of life can produce higher forms unless the higher is already at work effecting transformations within the lower. Man is a child of nature just as much as the lower forms of life in the vegetable and animal kingdoms. There is that, then, in nature capable of producing persons. It would follow, therefore, that there are forces in nature higher than the personal forces found in man. They may be super-personal, but they cannot be less than personal. These transcendent forces would be qualities or aspects of God. The two preceding arguments have considerable weight in establishing the fact of higher intelligence. The argument of existence in persons might also be used to establish the goodness and righteousness of God as well as his intelligence, for just as it may be argued that the lower of itself cannot produce the higher in the realm of intelligence, so the lower of itself cannot produce the higher in the realm of moral character. Righteousness which men observe in their fellows, and supremely for Christians in the person of Jesus Christ, suggests that God cannot be less good than Jesus Christ. The fact of Christ in the world suggests forces of righteousness in the universe upon which he drew to realize his own moral perfection.

[1] *Science and Religion,* p. 232.

The fourth consideration that supports belief in God may be called the pragmatic argument. Briefly stated the argument is that to live on the basis of belief in God works out better than to live as if there were no God. In the lives of the sincerely devout, belief in God seems to make a vital difference. Such lives for the most part are better integrated and better poised than are the lives of those who reject such belief. Belief in God invests life with meaning. One may not be able to comprehend that meaning or give it definite expression, but so long as he has the assurance that there is a larger meaning to which his own life and mission are adjusted, his life acquires a sense of significance which it would not have otherwise. As Walter Marshall Horton declares, to be a complete atheist means that there is nothing in life worth devoting oneself to. When, however, men do devote themselves to high causes in which presumably God himself is interested, they frequently have the experience of being in fellowship with forces greater than themselves which reinforce their own higher impulses and enable them to achieve beyond what they would deem possible if they had to depend on their own unaided strength. The sense of harmony with the central purpose or meaning of existence, and the sense of reinforcement of one's own limited powers which has been experienced by great numbers of those who have lived on the basis of faith in God, may be accepted as evidence that such faith is not in vain and that there is a transcendent reality which answers this outreach of the human spirit.

There are those also of mystical temperament who testify that they have experienced an actual union with God which leaves absolutely no doubt in their minds about the reality of his existence. How much value to attach to such testimony is difficult to determine because of the difficulty of submitting any such experience to an adequate test. Men with very contradictory ideas about the nature of God have had this experience of losing the sense of self in a temporary absorption into the sense of the infinite. Various means and methods have been used of inducing this state of mind, and wide and varied have been the interpretations given to the experience. An experience which can be induced by means of a Bacchic frenzy, or a tribal dance, or by the practices of Hindu yoga can hardly be accepted as valid evidence of the existence of God as he is conceived by Christians. However valuable the mystic experience may be to the individual, its nature is not such as to make it an argument that carries general conviction. The pragmatic argument, however, that sincere belief in God worthily conceived tends to result in a higher and more satisfactory type of life than its opposite, is a proposition which can be checked in human experience and to the practical mind should carry a good deal of weight.

GOD IN HISTORY

Another argument for the existence of God which is receiving increasing attention from thinkers of this generation may be designated as the judgment of history. This view holds that the working of God is evident in the historical process in two ways, which probably are best conceived as the obverse sides of a single process. The negative aspect of God's activity as revealed in history is judgment in the sense of condemnation and the sentence of destruction upon those institutions of life which persist in denying or thwarting the coming to being of a higher and more inclusive human fellowship. Institutions which stand in the way of justice and those which subordinate human values to personal ambitions or to economic and political ends, sooner or later come to destruction. The very nature of the moral order seems to guarantee this. The fact that social evils contain within themselves the seeds of their own destruction does not mean the absence of judgment, but rather that it is inherent in the social process. Judgment does not depend upon particular and arbitrary decisions of God in specific cases, but is wrought into the very structure of the world. An order of life in which judgment is integrated as an essential part is a divine order. God has ordained its character even though he does not determine the specific methods by which evil destroys itself in particular cases. The fact of judgment operating quite impersonally and independently in the historical process justifies a belief in God who controls the direction of history through the means of a moral order which he has ordained.

The positive aspect of God's activity in history is evident in those trends which bring men into closer relationships with one another despite themselves and their wishes in the matter. New developments of life increase the number of contacts between men so that groups and nations are being forced into closer relations with ane another. Situations are constantly being created in which the alternatives are an increase in mutual understanding and co-operation for the more inclusive good, or strife and destruction in the effort to maintain the older and lesser good. The pressure of events invites men on the one hand to move forward into a higher and more inclusive brotherhood in which the bonds of love will be greatly extended, or threatens them on the other hand with tribulation and suffering if they refuse to enter into this new opportunity when the stage is set. Professor H. N. Wieman declares that the evident trend in the world toward increasing interdependence represents a direct manifestation of the activity of God. "To discern this deep organic community of need and interdependence by which all men are bound together," he states, "is to discern the subtle and intricate weaving of the world process by which a web of ever-increasing interdependence is woven silently, secretly, pervasively, through all the doings of men and the workings of the universe. Men are being caught in a net of increasing interdependence which they themselves never intended to weave, against which they sometimes violently struggle, to which they are always more or less indifferent, but which mightily and persistently develops. . . . We are entangled in the bonds of love and cannot escape, struggle as we may."[2]

Man is constantly being confronted with the choice of entering voluntarily into these new opportunities for the expression of justice and love in larger dimensions, or of endeavoring to maintain the status quo at the risk of disaster. If he does not freely enter into the new opportunities to which he is invited by the trend of events, he will be battered and badgered through processes of destructive judgment into a recognition of the necessity of determining life on the basis of the higher morality demanded by the new situations. It would appear that God would prefer to lead men into his kingdom, but if they will not be led, they will be maneuvered at great social cost into situations where they will be forced to recognize that no social order can prevail in this world which is not founded upon righteousness, justice, and love. The pressure evident in new developments of life toward a better social order is interpreted as the work of God in history.

---

[2] *Methods of Private Religious Living,* pp. 78-79.

CHAPTER VII

Jesus Christ, the Son and the Saviour

I. In Relation to God

THE SON OF GOD

WHEN Christians are asked what is the relation of Jesus to God, the most frequent answer is that Jesus is the Son of God. In support of this answer they will cite, perhaps, the testimony of the voice from heaven at the time of his baptism which declared, "Thou art my beloved Son, in thee I am well pleased." Or they may refer to the similar testimony of the voice out of the cloud at the mountaintop transfiguration experience, "This is my beloved Son; hear ye him." The opening verse of Mark, the earliest Gospel, reads: "The beginning of the gospel of Jesus Christ, the Son of God." In the first three Gospels Jesus frequently speaks of God as "My Father" in a way that leaves no doubt that he believed himself to be in intimate filial relationship with God. The Gospel of John puts great stress on Jesus Christ as "the only begotten Son" and sums up the purpose of the entire work in saying, "These are written, that ye may believe that Jesus is the Christ, the Son of God; and that believing ye may have life in his name." (20:31.) The affirmation that Jesus Christ is the Son of God has always stood at the very center of Christian faith.

If, however, the question is asked, just what is meant when it is affirmed that Jesus is the Son of God, there is no unanimity among the answers. Many will affirm that Jesus is God's Son in a biological sense, that he had no human father, but was conceived by the Virgin Mary through the power of the Holy Spirit rather than by the normal process of human generation. Such is the testimony of two of the Gospels and this belief seems to have prevailed throughout the early Christian Church.

Many will also affirm that Jesus was God's Son prior to his advent on this earth, that he enjoyed a pre-existence with God as his Son in heaven and that he emptied himself of this exalted position to be born on earth as a human being. This attitude finds expression in the Epistles of Paul, especially in the letters to the Colossians, Ephesians, and Philippians. In the Colossians he speaks of Christ as "the image of the invisible God, the firstborn of all creation" through whom all things both in the heavens and on the earth were created. (Col. 1:15-17.) In the same discussion he asserts, "in him dwelleth all the fullness of the Godhead bodily" (2:9), by which he seems to say that there is no power in God which is not also found in Jesus Christ the Son. In his letter to the Philippians he again makes strong affirmation of the Son's equality with God, at least in his prehuman state, declaring, "who, existing in the form of God, counted not the being on an equality of God a thing to be grasped, but emptied himself, taking the form of a servant, being made in the likeness of men." (2:6, 7.)

The Gospel of John likewise identifies Christ with the creative Word, or Logos of God, through whom all things were created and in whom all things find life. "The Word became flesh and dwelt among us, full of grace and truth." (John 1:14.) The unity of Christ with God is asserted frequently throughout the Gospel.

In the light of the expanded universe which we of the twentieth century have had revealed to us, many people find it difficult, however, to find much vital meaning in such affirmations of the metaphysical union between the human Jesus of Nazareth and the God of the infinite expanses of space, whose creative activity proceeds before our very eyes. Fortunately for such as these it can be affirmed with confidence that this is not the heart of the matter for Christian faith.

Above all else what Christians mean when they assert the divine Sonship of Jesus Christ is a union of Christ with God in the realm of moral character. Jesus is the Son of God because of his moral likeness to God. As men become familiar with the qualities of the character of

Christ, they grow increasingly certain that the character of God is like that of Jesus, hence they declare him to be God's Son. If the moral character of Jesus did not carry conviction at this point, no amount of evidence in other realms would convince us that Jesus was worthy of the title, the Son of God. No story of a miraculous birth, no voices out of heaven, no affirmation of a Holy Book would convince us that Jesus was worthy of the reverence due to the Son of God, if his own moral character fell short of what we are ready to acknowledge as true of God. It is precisely because men marvel at the perfection of his character, and are ready to assert that if the God of the universe has a character like unto that of the human Jesus, he is worthy of our highest praise and love, that Christians designate Jesus as the Son of God. All other arguments are at least subsidiary to this one, if not indeed superfluous.

> If Jesus Christ is a man,—
>   And only a man,—I say
> That of all mankind I cleave to him,
>   And to him I will cleave alway.
>
> If Jesus Christ is a god,—
>   And the only God,—I swear
> I will follow Him through heaven and hell,
>   The earth, the sea, and the air![1]

THE REVELATION OF GOD

Another familiar designation for Jesus, "The Supreme Revelation of God," suggests the question, What is it that Jesus reveals to us about God? Among the functions commonly ascribed to God are those of the Creator, the Ruler and Sustainer of Nature. Does Jesus reveal God the Creator of the universe and of our world? Can one learn the steps in the process of creation by a study of the life and work and teachings of Jesus? Obviously not. If one wants dependable knowledge about such things he must go to the appropriate sciences such as geology and astronomy. Do we fare better when we seek information about the laws of nature's operation? Again we look in vain to the life and teachings

---

[1] "The Song of a Heathen," Richard Watson Gilder. Taken from Hill, *The World's Great Religious Poetry*, p. 323.

of Jesus, and find we must consult the natural sciences. A study of the sciences will teach us some important truths about the nature of God and his relation to nature that we do not find in Jesus. But if we do not find revealed in Jesus, God, the Creator, or God, the Ruler of Nature, what God does he reveal? The Christian answers, "He reveals God, the Father." His revelation has not to do with God in his impersonal operations but in his personal relations. Jesus reveals the heart of God, his inner character. The personal qualities of God can be made plain only through the medium of a personal revelation. Jesus is that revelation.

SCIENTIFIC REVELATIONS INADEQUATE

A religion which had to depend solely on the revelations of God that emerge from an understanding of scientific truth would be barren, indeed. When we have learned all that the natural sciences can tell us of God, we have only the evidence of a great and mighty power that works in dependable and orderly fashion in creating, sustaining, and ruling the universe. Whether God is personal as well as impersonal, natural science cannot tell us. Whether he is motivated by love for men, it cannot say with any assurance. What is the standing of man in the mind of God, it knows not. What are the high and abiding values to be realized in life? What is the purpose of creation, the meaning of life, and the destiny of man? Before such questions the natural sciences are dumb. As far as they are concerned the nature of God's moral character remains an enigma. The god which science reveals might call forth from us awe and dread, but love him we could not.

The most important thing to know about any person, if you would really know him, is the nature of his spirit, or moral character. We may know many things about a person, but if this knowledge is lacking, we do not truly know him. We may know of his physical strength, his intellectual ability, his special gifts, his success in a business or a profession, and yet be ignorant of that which is most important about him, his character. All these other things might be known without knowing the motives which dominate his action, his ideals and aspirations, inner purposes, or principles of conduct. Just such would be our plight with respect to God if we had to depend upon the sciences for our knowledge of him.

There are those who affirm that the gospel of nature is enough for them, that in the worship of the woods and flowers, sea and sky, mountains and lakes, the requirements of their souls are met. This is a great fallacy for the very reason that the things we most need to know are not revealed in impersonal nature, that is, in nature exclusive of its human manifestations. There is nothing in objective nature which tells us with any degree of assurance what is God's attitude toward man. Nothing tells us what place man has in the divine plans and purposes or with what worth he is endowed by the Creator. Science does not tell us whether God loves us, or is merely indifferent to our presence. For all that nature tells us we may be mere puppets made by the Creator for his amusement. It is not nature that assures us that God loves individuals with a love that transcends human love. Nature does not tell us whether God cares anything about human suffering, or whether our longings and aspirations mean anything to him. Is righteousness anything more than human expediency? Does it possess more than temporary virtue? This nature does not reveal. These concerns are related to the inner character of God, to his fundamental desires, purposes and attitudes, and such qualities of spirit can only be revealed through that which is personal.

Jesus is the supreme revelation of God because he brings to light that which we most need to know about God, his inner character. With Jesus in the world it is possible to make many affirmations about the ultimate character of the universe that would not be possible without him. As a stream cannot rise higher than its source, so those forces which produced him must be at least as righteous, and good, and loving as he. God cannot be less in moral character than Jesus. It is in him that we learn of God's amazing love for men, and his high purposes for them. It is from him that we learn the worth of a human soul. In his life of service we see revealed God's righteousness and beneficence, and in his death upon the cross we see the heart of God, suffering that he may reconcile man to himself. Only in Christ do we find so full and so significant a revelation.

One marvels at the growing discovery of God on the part of the Hebrew people as related in the Old Testament and especially as found in their great men of God, the prophets. But sum up the revelation of all these seers and it falls short both in quality and proportion to the revelation of Jesus Christ. Today we correct the imperfect conceptions of the character of God in the Old Testament by Jesus as the standard. Although the Old Testament is cherished as a wonderful record of religious experience and insight, and for its developing revelation of God, it pales in meaning for us in the light of the New Testament, because the latter is the book of Jesus Christ.

God, although invisible, has not left himself without a witness. It is as though a writer were seeking information for a biography for a noble figure who had passed on. He goes to the community where the man lived and makes inquiries about him. He is told that the deceased has a son living whose spirit is just like that of the father and would he learn of the father the best and quickest way is to cultivate an intimate knowledge of the son. So Christians who would know the character of God seek to further their knowledge of Jesus Christ, for as Henry Sloane Coffin has declared, "Our conceptions of the Most High God are forever being revised in order to make the Father whom we worship as good as his Son."

II. IN RELATION TO MEN

THE SAVIOUR

When attention is turned from the relation of Jesus to God to his relation to men, other titles are preferred to designate the nature of the relationship such as, Lord, Master, the Great Physician, the Elder Brother, the Good Shepherd. The most important of these titles, however, from the standpoint of Christian doctrine, is "The Saviour of Men." As we found it necessary to seek the essential meaning of the term "Son of God," so we must ask how does Jesus effect the salvation of men.

As Christians endeavor to explain the process of Christian salvation they tend to divide in various camps representing various theories. In this discussion no attempt will be made to consider all the variants, but an effort will be made to indicate the poles of thought between which the ideas of Christians tend to oscillate.

It is impossible to consider the problem of Jesus in relation to other men without facing more fully the question of his own essential nature. There are those who declare that the Saviour of men must be more-than-human in his nature; that one who was only human would not be competent for so high a function. He who would be a Saviour must be divine in his nature in a way that no person who was only human could be. It is not denied that he must be human, but unless his nature transcends the human he would be incompetent to perform the saving mission. These people would assert, therefore, that Jesus was both God and man, not simply in the way of identification of moral character such as was described above, but in a way quite unique. Jesus was a God-man, possessing not one single nature but two, a divine nature and a human nature which dwelt in juxtaposition with one another. If we may take the Westminster Confession of Faith, which was adopted in A.D. 1647, as typical of the official creeds of the churches, its statement concerning the nature of Christ will be found of interest:

The Son of God, the second person in the Trinity, being very and eternal God, of one substance, and equal with the Father, did, when the fullness of time was come, take upon him man's nature with all the essential properties and common infirmities thereof, yet without sin: being conceived by the power of the Holy Ghost in the womb of the Virgin Mary, of her substance. So that two whole, perfect, and distinct natures, the Godhood and the manhood, were inseparably joined together in one person, without conversion, composition, or confusion. Which person is very God and very man, yet one Christ, the only mediator between God and man.

If the question is raised, "How can such things be?" the only answer that can be given is that it is a part of the divine mystery. It is above human understanding and therefore cannot be explained in terms that are rational for us.

If, however, the question asked is, "Why must the Saviour possess a dual nature?" an understandable answer is presented. The fundamental assumption on which the whole explanation rests is that before God can forgive men their offenses and restore them to divine favor and fellowship, it is necessary that the requirements of divine justice be fulfilled. Thinking in terms of Old Testament practices the propitiation of sins requires sacrifices on the part of the sinner. But the ancient sacrifices could be only partially availing, mere gestures as it were of man's desire for reconciliation with God. The reason for this was that man in his offenses had sinned against an Infinite God and this made the offense infinite in quality calling for a sacrifice likewise of infinite worth.

Man being a finite creature and sinful could not possibly offer such a
sacrifice. Therefore left to himself his case was utterly hopeless; he
could not provide for his own salvation. Provisions must be made by
God himself, or man was forever lost. God himself, therefore, as an
act of great mercy, evolved a plan that would fulfill all the requirements
of divine justice and accomplish man's salvation. The plan called for
his sending his only-begotten Son to the earth to be born in the form
of a man with a human nature, without, however, the loss of his divine
nature. As a true human being he could act in behalf of the human
race. As one who was both sinless and divine he could offer himself as
a sacrifice of infinite worth and so blot out man's obligation to God.
This he did by his death on the cross. Because he was both man and
God he could accomplish for man what man could not do for himself
and open the way for divine forgiveness and reconciliation. It remains
only for man by an act of faith to accept the salvation that Christ has
wrought. This program is known as the substitutionary theory of the
atonement and forms the basis for all conservative, or "orthodox" views
of Christian salvation.

Advocates of the substitutionary view make much of the evidences
in the New Testament that point to a unique nature in the case of
Jesus Christ, especially those that suggest supernatural qualities. The
record of the Virgin Birth is especially prized because it provides an
account of how one essential to the carrying out of this theory was met.
If Christ had been born as a result of the ordinary processes of human
generation, he would have inherited an increment of original sin which
would have unfitted him for making an infinite sacrifice. Only one
who was sinless in his nature as well as in act could render such a sacrifice. All the posterity of Adam inherit a corrupted human nature. By
reason of his supernatural generation, Jesus escaped all sinful taint and
predisposition in his nature. On the other hand, as a result of being
born of woman he was truly man and could assume upon himself the
burden of man's guilt. Jesus' miracles, and especially the nature miracles, are also accepted as evidences of his Godhood, as is also his resurrection from the dead. Death had no dominion over him because he
was God. While it can still be maintained that the most essential element in Jesus' Sonship to God was his likeness to God in moral char-

acter, this theory requires also the assertion of Jesus' deity in a sense impossible to any other human being.

A LIBERAL CRITICISM

Christians of more liberal or left-wing tendencies do not find the substitutionary theory a satisfactory explanation of Christ's saving work. They criticize it as being founded on a legal fiction and as not picturing truly God's relationship to man. They question the whole assumption that the divine justice requires a legalistic satisfaction. God's relation to men is not that of an exalted and exacting judge jealous of the fine points of his legal system, but is that of a loving Father, even as Jesus presented him in his teachings. To discover what God requires of men as the basis of reconciliation we must ask not what a judge would demand of offenders against a system of legal justice, but what a father would require of wayward children. The clearest answer to the latter question is found in Jesus' Parable of the Prodigal Son (Lk. 15:11–32), a story of a son who separated himself from his father in order to give expression to his own sinful desires, and of a reconciliation when the son discovered the great error of his life and with changed heart and purpose returned to the father's house. Legal requirements find no place in the picture. What one is made to see with simple clarity is the picture of a father whose loving heart yearns for the return of his wayward son. At the same time the son knows that he cannot return and claim any favor from his father until he is ready to recognize the error of his own way and determines henceforth to live according to the wiser and better way of his father's household. Such a change of heart and mind constitutes the very essence of repentance. According to Jesus' story the only necessity for a complete restoration of the son to a place of fellowship and favor was a sincere repentance. Every time a sinner repents and seeks forgiveness there is great joy in the presence of God; it becomes an occasion of heavenly rejoicing.

REVELATION THEORY

If the father-son relationship as depicted in this story of the Forgiving Father prevails between man and God, the question may well be asked, wherein then lies the need for a Saviour. The answer is that man needs a revelation of what constitutes the Father's will and way for human life. Jesus Christ is that revelation. By perfect submission of himself to what he discerned to be God's will for human life he has made the divine purpose manifest. No longer need man be in doubt concerning the way of life which meets with the favor of God. Jesus has made it plain. Moreover, he has demonstrated what human life may become when men learn to live as true sons of God. The triumphant life which he lived was not achieved through his own unaided power as a man, but was attained through laying hold of the power and resources of God. As an essential part of his revelation he has made clear the conditions under which the energies of God may be released in human life to the end of making life abundant.

When Jesus summoned men to follow him, to become his disciples, he was not asking them merely to follow his example in outward manner or incidental matters. Nor was he inviting them to achieve spiritual victory through pulling themselves up by their moral bootstraps. He challenged them rather to commit their lives to the same great ends and purposes to which he gave his life, to dedicate themselves without reserve to the program and way of God in the world, in the assurance that to the extent that they would make such dedication in sincerity, the energies of God that found release and expression through him would also find release through them. They could become agents of divine powers even as he had, and on the same terms. The saints, those who have been recognized as great men of God throughout the ages, have with one voice acknowledged that they achieved their work not through their own strength, but as instruments of a power mightier than they. This is what Jesus promises to all those who will follow him in complete commitment of themselves to the purposes and program of God as he makes it plain.

An outstanding representative of the liberal view of Christ's saving work is Dr. Harry Emerson Fosdick. In this connection he has said: "The Spirit of God in Jesus made his quality; that same spirit is underground in our lives, striving to well up in characters like his, until we live, yet not we but Christ lives in us." Another modern interpreter of the meaning of Jesus, Mary Ely Lyman, has said: "Faith in the power of God to bring to pass the highest that we know in ideal becomes ours through Jesus' revelation of God's power working in him. Jesus led men to God. . . . Our appeal to him today is not for authority, but for the quickening of our life with God through the revelation that he gave of how a human life can reflect and be filled with God's life."[2]

For those who accept the view of Christ's saving work being done through the medium of such a revelation of how to live by the power of God, the older view of Christ's dual nature becomes more of a stumbling block than a help. To ascribe to Christ a nature that other men cannot and do not possess is to place other men under an impossible handicap so far as attaining to his moral and spiritual likeness is concerned. It would have little meaning to challenge men to follow Christ if he is essentially a different kind of being by nature than they are. This school, therefore, emphasizes the essential humanity of a Christ whose divinity represents a moral achievement. Enough for them that Christ represents a moral identity with God, not a complete metaphysical oneness that would assert that in Jesus Christ dwelt the fullness of the Godhead bodily. The miraculous element in the New Testament is minimized as a part of the temporary framework of thought within which the portrait of Christ had to be drawn, as his age was a prescientific one which thought naturally in terms of miraculous action. Those miracles which cannot be accounted for on rational grounds in the light of the fuller knowledge of our day are usually credited to the tendency for a miracle tradition to grow up around a great figure who made a remarkable impress on the life of his age in pre-scientific times. It should be added, however, there is a considerable tendency to affirm, in the light of Jesus' most unusual attainment in the realm of character and filial relationship to God, that achievements would be possible to him through perfectly natural means which would be beyond the power of lesser men. Even the most modern of interpreters of Jesus would be slow to affirm that they fully comprehend his nature. Whether by endowment, as the more conservative affirm, or by attainment, as liberals would assert, there is that about him which transcends ordinary human categories.

[2] *Jesus*, p. 54.

CHAPTER VIII

The New Realism about Sin

PRIOR to World War I, Christian liberalism seemed to be coming into its own. It was very optimistic about the improvement of man and of his world and the possibility of realizing the Kingdom of God on earth at an early date. It was inclined to regard sin as a compound of error and ignorance which could be overcome by more efficient and universal education. It was believed that man was essentially good and all he needed was sufficient enlightenment as to the method of achieving the good. Sin became an unpopular subject, an outmoded category of thought, which served no useful purpose in the new day of social intelligence. By improving of environmental conditions under which the new generation was growing up and by providing an adequate program of education for all youth, it was believed possible to produce a generation that would set the world's wrongs right and realize something of a Utopia. Then came the first World War! It was a shock, to be sure, to the optimistic faith of these liberals; but they were inclined to interpret it as the last stand of forces of evil against the onward march of intelligent righteousness. Evil would defeat itself and the ground would be clear for the rapid building of the Kingdom of Righteousness. So the romanticism of many Christians, in America at least, survived the terrors of the holocaust. A wave of enthusiastic expectation spread through the country following the war, looking toward the establishment of a glorious new order in the relation of men and nations. Instead of seeing these expectations realized, however, years of disillusionment followed as democracies were disrupted by forces of corruption and were subjected to reigns of terror. The economic system, which was to provide abundantly the material needs of the new order, broke down in its operation and the world was plunged into the worst depression of its history, reducing great masses of people to desperation. Nations which had promised to disarm and live peaceably with one another proceeded to build vast armaments beyond anything ever known in peacetime history and World War II followed, the horrors and destructiveness of which were ghastly beyond description. Instead of the Kingdom of Righteousness the Kingdom of Evil seems to have triumphed in the world. These disillusionments of history, so in contrast with the expectations of a generation ago, have given rise to a new realism with respect to human nature, and have made men acutely conscious of the problem of sin.

Sin has been variously defined by Christian thinkers. According to the Westminster Shorter Catechism, sin is "any want of conformity unto, or transgression of, the law of God." If we turn to a Catholic catechism, we find an important modification in that sin is defined as "a willful transgression of the law of God." In the New Testament, the Book of James, we read "to him that knoweth to do good and doeth it not, it is sin." (James 4:17.) This latter statement would seem to say that sin is failure to follow what is recognized as the better of two or more alternative modes of action. Man sins when he chooses not to live according to the best he knows, when he knowingly accepts the worse rather than the better course of action.

Before proceeding further with a discussion of these views, it will be helpful to make clear the distinction between two terms that are often confused in the minds of people, namely, sin and evil. Evil is the more comprehensive term and can be identified with anything which militates against the highest interests of life. It includes various natural phenomena, such as earthquakes, floods, damage by lightning, cyclones and tornadoes, and destructive fires, disease and plagues. The evil effects of such forces are easily apparent, but to the extent that they are not directly related to the moral failure of human beings, they cannot be regarded as sin. We must recognize, also, social environments which are evil in their effects upon those who are forced to live within them. They may have arisen as a consequence of human moral failures, but their evil effects fall upon those who may be completely innocent so far as contributing to the rise of such conditions. For the guiltless these conditions represent evil, not sin. Sin, however it may be defined, always refers to human moral failure. Thus all sin is evil, but not all evil is sin.

THE STATE OF SIN

We have been speaking of sin in terms of definite moral failures, but it is important to note that the term is sometimes used in another sense, referring to a state or condition of the soul. According to the views of traditional orthodoxy, the first parents of the human race were placed in an earthly paradise in a state of complete innocence, and all that was required of them in return for the blessings of this paradise was complete obedience to the rules God had established. These original humans were endowed with freedom of choice and under the temptation of Satan in the form of a serpent, they ate of the forbidden fruit of the garden and in this act of disobedience were guilty of sin against God. As a result of this disobedience they fell from their state of innocency and their natures became corrupt, that is, they became predisposed to sin rather than goodness. Inasmuch as they were the progenitors of the entire human race, all of their descendants inherited this corruption of nature and are said to dwell in a state of sin. This belief is known as the doctrine of natural depravity. Many thinkers have held that as a result of this fall from a state of innocency and natural goodness, man's nature became wholly corrupt and completely inclined to evil, and so incapable of any good. From this state of original sin proceed all actual transgressions. Conveyed from one generation to another through the process of ordinary generation, it is held that men are born in a state of sin. How seriously this doctrine has been taken in times past by some earnest believers is illustrated in "An Address to the Rising Generation" which was delivered to children by Rev. John Brown, minister of the Gospel at Haddington, and published in 1764 together with two short catechisms. In this address he admonishes children in a way that would be thought criminal by most modern educators:

Oh! think, seriously think, how deplorable is your natural estate? In Adam you all "have sinned; ye are of your father the devil, and the lusts of your father you will do." "You are children of disobedience, children of wrath, even as others." Your "carnal mind is enmity against God, and is not subject to his law, neither indeed can be:" your heart is hard as adamant; "is filled with all unrighteousness, wickedness" and malignity; is deceitful above all things, and desperately wicked; an habitation of devils, and of every unclean and hateful lust; and out of it proceed "evil thoughts, murders, adulteries, fornications, thefts, false witness, blasphemies." Ah! Thy shocking vileness! "wilt thou not be made clean? When shall it once be?" With horror think how much of life you have already cast away in the practice of sin.

Not all those who have accepted the doctrine of original sin have held, however, the doctrine of the total depravity of human nature. Many have believed that by the act of disobedience of Adam and Eve, human nature simply became infected with sin and so incapable of living a life wholly righteous and free from guilt. Man faces life not altogether incapable of good but on the other hand, not capable of a complete goodness, and, therefore, a bondservant to sin. As such he is under the wrath of God and must suffer the punishments ordained for sinners unless he avails himself of the means of redemption which God has provided.

STATUTORY VIEW OF SIN

Those definitions of sin which held it to be "any want of conformity unto, or transgression of, the law of God" or "a willful transgression of the law of God" conceive of sin in a legalistic or statutory manner. The assumption is that God has ordained a code of laws governing all the acts of man. Had not man fallen from his original state of favor, he would have been fully informed of God's requirements. As it is, a revelation of God's moral law has been given for man's guidance in the Bible. This, of course, can only be known by those who have had direct contact with the Christian tradition. The essence of sin according to these definitions is a transgression at any point of this divine law. There is a very important difference, however, between these two statements, for the first one makes any transgression whatsoever a sin, while the second declares that it must be a willful transgression. According to the first view ignorance is no excuse before the law even though one has never had opportunity to know the requirements of the law. Uninstructed heathen are as guilty and as much under the wrath of God as are those who know the law and still violate it. In the early phases of the Protestant missionary movement, one of the most powerful motives in the inciting to missionary activity was the prospect of millions of heathen destined for eternal damnation because of never having heard the gospel of redemption. Missionaries went forth with the purpose of plucking as many brands as possible from the burning.

According to the second view only a willful transgression involves guilt which means, of course, that a man must be capable of recognizing the violation as such. Failure to make use of one's opportunities to know the divine law would, of course, be one of the most serious and fundamental sins, but a truly innocent act of transgression of the divine law would not involve guilt, nor deserve a penalty other than the natural consequences of the evil involved. The moral penalties to be suffered would correspond to the degree of a man's guilt. The ultimate destiny of the unredeemed would be the same in either case, but for the redeemed the penalties to be suffered for violations of the divine law would be in strict accord with the extent of man's willful transgressions. The consequences of sin, therefore, according to these statutory views are the suffering of the punishments which God has prepared for sinners, and for the unforgiven the final consequence is damnation in a hell of eternal suffering. For the redeemed the punishments may take the form of various types of misfortunes, both spiritual and material.

DEGRADATION VIEW

When sin is regarded as a choice of the lesser rather than the better good, or of the worse rather than the better alternative of action, the basis becomes one of conscience rather than the violation of statutes. Moral responsibility is an important aspect of this view. One must know the right or at least have had opportunity to know the right if he is to be held accountable for doing the right. Sin is failure to do the right according to one's highest insights. This may seem to water down the conception and diminish the seriousness of offenses, but the seriousness of the offense is determined by the degree of variation between actual conduct and what one recognizes as ideal conduct. In some instances this is slight, but in very many instances it is marked. One has only to look into his own life to realize that all are guilty of sin, for none of us succeeds in living up to the best that we recognize.

Many of the worst evils against which mankind must struggle are the direct results of man's deliberate choice of inferior ways of conduct.

The Apostle Paul in his epistle to the Galatians gave a list of important sins of his day which he termed works of the flesh, the practice of which would disqualify one for the Kingdom of God. He includes "fornication, uncleanness, lasciviousness, idolatry, sorcery, enmities, strife, jealousies, wraths, factions, divisions, parties, envyings, drunkenness, revellings, and such like." (5:19–21.) Such sins are still with us, playing havoc in the lives of individuals, families, and communities.

In the ages since, however, with the increasing organization and complexity of life, sin has taken on many new and additional forms and we are required to greatly expand Paul's catalogue. Ours is a corporate age in which the work and activities of life are carried on not by isolated individuals or small intimate groups, but by great organizations of men in corporations, associations, and institutions. The new forms of sin belonging to our age include various types of industrial pressure such as child labor, beating down wages, maintaining sweatshop conditions, failure to take safety measures, interference with labor organization, inciting to violence, sabotage, cut-throat competition and racketeering. In connection with the distribution of the products of industry, we encounter misrepresentation of goods, lying advertising, charging all the traffic will bear, and taking inordinate profits. In the realm of government we contend with political graft and corruption, national imperialisms, and war. In the field of race relations there are various types of unfair discrimination, both social and economic, frequently finding expression in mob action. We find also in our midst organized prostitution, and the debasing of public morals through pandering to the lowest of human impulses for private gain. Corporations have been known to promote international ill-will and suspicion for the sake of increased dividends resulting from the sales of armaments, and nations have been plunged into war at the cost of millions of lives for the sake of protecting their financial advantages. There is general recognition among intelligent people that these modes of action represent inferior kinds of conduct and are, therefore, sins; but the responsibility for such policies is so diffused that it is exceedingly difficult to fix the blame. These corporate sins are very far-reaching in their effects and often-times more destructive of the good than the private sins of individuals. Their complexity makes them extremely difficult to deal with and to eradicate, and for this reason the problem of sin grows more rather than less important with the increasing interdependence of life.

CONSEQUENCES FOR THE EVILDOER

While it is apparent that sins, whether individual or social, leave a train of evils in their wake from which all society suffers, it is important to note also the consequence of sin in the character of the sinner. According to the degradation view the result of sin is moral deterioration. Through choosing the worse rather than the better alternative of action, one tends to dull his sensitivities to the distinctions between the good and the bad. Because it is human to try always to rationalize one's conduct the second offense never seems nearly so bad as the first, and through repeated offenses one can dull his conscience in that particular regard until the sense of wrong is practically lost. Repeated choices of the evil over the good in a widening area of activities may eventually result in the loss of ability to distinguish between right and wrong and the acquisition of a perverted scale of moral values. On the other hand, persistence in following the better alternatives tends to sharpen one's moral discriminations and to sensitize his conscience. It is noteworthy that the keenest sense of sin is to be found among people of most saintly character, the dullest sense among persistent offenders against the good. Some would argue that a keen conscience is a disadvantage in a world like this. If, however, the universe is fundamentally moral in its character, then to continue to live in it with a wholly perverted sense of moral values is impossible. This would mean defying the trend to nature itself. He who attempts it makes a hell for himself, for the very order of existence denies him the satisfaction which he seeks. The ultimate consequence of contending against the moral order is to be crushed by that order. The wages of sin is death.

ORIGINAL NATURE OF MAN

Those who follow the degradation view of sin are very apt to disagree with those who accept a statutory view with respect to the original nature of man. They do not conceive of man having lived originally in a state of perfect righteousness from which he has fallen into a state of natural corruption. They are more inclined to accept the verdict of the science of psychology with respect to the quality of man's inherited nature. On this basis it is maintained that the native equipment with which man begins life is neither good nor evil. Man is endowed with certain inherent urges, seeking expression in activity. They are capable of expression in ways that are good and in ways that are harmful. The way that life is conditioned by environmental influences will largely determine whether these primary urges express themselves in constructive or destructive ways. In themselves they are morally neutral. It may be granted that in the evolutionary development of man the more egoistic impulses developed first and are more deeply embedded in his nature than the more social and altruistic impulses which are more recent and not so highly developed.

In so far as human beings begin life as self-centered individuals it can be said that by nature they are predisposed to sin. If this be true, man's biological nature is still somewhat faulty as a basis upon which to realize the life of unselfish goodness. These obstacles which inhere in man's biological inheritance might be regarded as the equivalent of original sin, but this could never be equated with total depravity.

SOCIAL EQUIVALENT OF ORIGINAL SIN

Much more importance is attached to social than to physical impediments to a life of complete goodness, for the pressure to accept the worse rather than the better alternative often comes from without a man in the form of social suggestion, or even coercion. Whenever evil becomes conventionalized and institutionalized, it is capable of exerting tremendous pressure in the direction of conformity upon the individual, even when he recognizes that the accepted customs do not represent the highest mode of action. A student who enters college with high ideals of sexual morality may find himself associated with a social group whose accepted practices are much lower than his own. He will find that it requires Herculean courage to maintain his own standards of action against the pressure of the group which always seeks conformity on the part of all its members. Many persons who would prefer not to drink alcoholic beverages, if left to their own wish in the matter, find themselves today in situations where it is all but impossible to refrain from indulgence. A man may even be working in behalf of a very worthy and good cause, but his task brings him in social contact with people who drink as a matter of course and regard as queer those who will not join them in a social glass. The champion of the good cause may find his case prejudiced if he refuses to drink with a group which he is seeking to influence. Rather than make his cause unpopular by prejudicing people against himself, he feels compelled to yield his own personal standard of action in order to secure the goodwill of the group which he is trying to influence to support a worthy project in another realm of life.

Honesty is said to be the best policy, but there are thousands of situations today both in the social and commercial worlds where absolute honesty is exceedingly costly and where to be "too honest" does not pay. In such situations the person committed to honesty may find the cost too great to maintain his honesty in a situation where a measure of dishonesty is required for success. Evil has always been expert in either idealizing itself or at least in rationalizing itself as the only practical course, and when it becomes established in the form of social conventions its force is almost irresistible. An individual employer may be aware of the evil of low wages in his industry, but unless he can persuade the entire industry to raise the wage level, he may find, if he attempts to break the established practice by raising wages in his plant, that he will in turn be broken by his competitors who in their resentment against his action will unite to bring about his destruction. The evils of life become institutionalized and virtually force individuals into accepting courses of action which as they readily recognize fall far short of the ideal. As compared with the impediment to good in our physical inheritance, these social impediments are veritable mountains. It is to the fact that evil is intrenched in society that man must look for the principal explanation of his predisposition to sin.

CORPORATE SIN AND THE JUDGMENT

Religion insists as one of its fundamental convictions upon the fact of moral judgment. We have already spoken of the views of judgment held by those who take the statutory view of sin and by those who hold the degradation view as applied to individual wrongdoers. But what about judgment of corporate sins? Is it possible that sin socially organized may succeed in a world where individual sin fails? If this is a moral universe then it will no more support public sin than private. It may require a longer time for judgment to operate, but institutions built upon unsound moral foundations contain inherent weaknesses which, despite temporary successes, destine them for eventual failure. One reason why they may resist distintegration for a long time is that corporate evils involve a high degree of co-operation. Co-operation is a virtue inasmuch as it seeks social goods over and above individual goods. But co-operation may be perverted to the service of ends less than the best, and when this happens it encourages the growth within itself of the seeds of its own destruction. Just because corporate sins represent a large admixture of good with the evil, they are more resistant to disintegrating forces, but as the evil grows it invites destruction upon both the good and the evil. A survey of history reveals that those institutions of life which obstructed progress toward the realization of the higher personal values of life have passed under condemnation, however powerful or deeply intrenched they once were. Human slavery, feudalism, terrors of the inquisition, witchcraft, and the regarding of women as personal property represent a few examples of institutions that have already passed off the stage in the interest of the larger and better life for man. Child labor, political and economic autocracy, and imperialistic war are other examples of institutions now under the judgment. It is of the very nature of religious faith to assert that a day of reckoning eventually overtakes every form of sin no matter how deeply rooted or how mixed with forms of good. Religion affirms its faith in a moral universe.

CHAPTER IX

Right and Wrong

ON SEVERAL occasions the author has asked his students in a discussion class on Religious Problems to write a paper comparable to a theme in freshman composition on how in any specific situation to determine the right from the wrong course of action. They were not asked to do any reading on the subject, but simply to think about the matter and write a summary of their own conclusions. When the assignment was made most of the students regarded it lightly as involving no particular difficulty; but if they really thought about the matter seriously, the more they considered it the more difficult it became to find a wholly satisfactory answer. The answers given were hotly debated in the class sessions.

When the responses were analyzed the sources of help and guidance in making moral decisions which were mentioned could be classified under four headings. The one usually mentioned first and most often was parental instruction. Others included the conscience, prevailing social standards, and the moral teachings of the Bible as taught by the churches. In the last group several specific standards were designated, such as, the Ten Commandments, the teachings of the prophets, and the example and teachings of Jesus. There were a very few who rather tenuously took the position that there are no guiding principles which have universal and permanent validity, so that the final decision is largely a matter of personal preference and expediency. The majority conviction, however, would be that the latter position leads only to moral chaos and that there must be at least some minimum of objective control to guide individuals into right rather than wrong action.

PARENTAL TRAINING

When the above-mentioned resources are subjected to criticism, while all are found to be of great value, some are subject to decided limitations as sufficient and trustworthy guides. Parental training, which includes the example set as well as the precepts taught, affects very deeply the attitudes of normal children. Fortunate are children whose home training is in accord with the highest moral ideals! But unfortunately this is not always the situation. Some children, for instance, are taught at home to lie about their true age in order to take advantage of public transportation companies, theaters and the like, in order to secure reduced fares or admissions to which they are not properly entitled, and are brought up to believe that petty deceits to further their own advantage are legitimate so long as they can avoid detection. Examples could easily be multiplied to show that the standards which dominate many homes fall far short of the best, and cannot be regarded as trustworthy guides. While it is always well for children to honor their parents, in some circumstances it becomes necessary for them to take exception to parental instruction in order to pursue the right.

CONSCIENCE

"Let your conscience be your guide" is a watchword frequently quoted as a directive in choosing right from wrong. Just what is meant by conscience is not altogether clear, although it refers to something very real in human experience. In common usage it refers to an inherent sense of right and wrong. It is not difficult to demonstrate, however, that our conceptions of what constitute right and wrong are learned, that is, through direct training and the impress on our minds of the standards that are accepted in the society about us particularly during the most formative period of character. Inasmuch as acts that are considered right in one society may be regarded as wrong in a quite different one individual consciences vary accordingly. In the light of this fact it cannot be asserted that man is equipped by nature with a mental device or instinct which instructs him in every or any situation as to the right or wrong way of action. It is a unique characteristic of the human species, however, that he is capable of forming moral judgments in the light of relevant considerations, and that he is impelled by a sense that he ought to do the right in every situation. When he denies the right as seen, as often he does, he is subject to a feeling of guilt, of self-condemnation, and to be condemned by oneself may be more disturbing and distasteful than to be condemned by others. The feeling of self-approval which follows upon doing the right as the individual perceives it, or of self-condemnation when the right is denied, is apparently the essence of conscience. In this sense it may be affirmed that one ought never to violate his conscience by doing that for which he will stand condemned in his own eyes. But who has not had the experience of acting in accord with what his conscience approved at the time, only to realize in the light of later perspective that actually what he did was wrong and to be regretted. Under such a situation he has not been guilty of sin, except on a narrowly legalistic view, nor should he be subject to remorse, but, nevertheless, his action was wrong rather than right. If thus it is conceded that conscience must itself be trained and educated by experience, it can scarcely function where real uncertainty exists as to what is the right or wrong mode of behavior. Uncertainty is the evidence that the conscience offers no clear guidance in a particular situation, and in such a circumstance it cannot be of much help. Our problem is how to determine right from wrong when the distinction is not clear.

SOCIAL STANDARDS

As a matter of fact for most people the most important factor in arriving at moral decisions is found in the accepted standards of one's dominant social group. All people live in relation to a number of different social groups, such as, the family, the neighborhood, an occupational group, a social and recreational group, a fraternal group perhaps, and a religious group. In his relations with all these groups the individual naturally desires their approval on his conduct rather than disapproval, but in cases of serious conflict in values he will be most deeply influenced by the standards of the group whose good opinion he prizes most highly. But actually, in many situations the action will be determined by the standards of the group exerting the most pressure on the individual at the time of making a decision, and the result may well be expressed in the familiar motto, "When in Rome, do as the Romans do."

In considering the advisability of permitting the immediate society to determine one's standards of conduct it is necessary to distinguish between incidental folkways that have no moral significance and real differences in moral values from society to society and culture to culture. The same principle may well be expressed in quite different ways from place to place. The protection of human life from unnecessary hazards is a moral obligation that is recognized generally. In line with this principle communities establish rules of the road and various traffic regulations. In this country traffic passes to the right; in England to the left. What is a correct mode of action here is wrong over there, not because of any difference over essential moral values, but because of differences in established human conventions. With respect to these conventions one ought to adapt himself to the ways of the society in which he finds himself so far as courtesy and the ability to get along with people require. So long as no compromise with one's own principles of conduct is required, it would seem proper to conform to the ways of the group with whom one may be associated.

There is a larger degree of agreement among people of various cultures as to the basic nature of right and wrong than is at first apparent when one considers the outward differences in modes of life. C. S. Lewis, the English layman, whose radio talks and books on religion have received world-wide acclaim, insists that different ages and civilizations are not marked by quite different moralities but by *"slightly* different moralities." "Just think what a *quite* different morality would mean," he suggests. "Think of a country where people were *admired* for running away in battle, or where a man felt proud for double-crossing all the people who had been kindest to him. You might as well try to imagine a country where two and two make five."[1] Examples can be multiplied of basic values that receive general recognition.

There are, however, important differences in the accepted values of various civilizations and societies and the question as to how far the standards of the individual should be determined by the prevailing ones of his immediate society is a real one. Only on the basis that one set of values is as true as another can it be maintained that the individual ought to conform in all matters to the accepted standards of

[1] *The Case for Christianity*, p. 5.

his society. On this basis Nazi values for people of Germany under the Hitler regime were as valid as democratic values for the people of the United States, as there would be no objective standard by which to choose between them. Moreover, every society has its own moral blindspots. While it may see clearly the faults of others, it may be quite indistinct with respect to its own. In this country the North sees the faults of the South, and the South of the North, more clearly than they see their own. Someone has said that the South loves Negroes individually but despises the race, whereas the North honors the race but despises its individual members. Both attitudes are wrong and this fact shows the need for some objective standard of right by which to judge the attitudes and actions of any society. At this point religion may have a contribution to make.

THE TEN COMMANDMENTS

High religion cannot rest satisfied with a position of complete relativity in morals. It claims to possess deeper moral insights than are expressed in prevailing standards and asserts its right to sit in judgment on accepted social practices. While it is a great social asset to have high moral ideals accepted generally and translated into standards of action, moral progress would cease if any set of prevailing standards, no matter how high, came to be accepted as furnishing adequate guidance with respect to right and wrong. Such progress takes place only as accepted patterns are criticized in the light of higher ideals, and to offer such criticism has been the function of prophets and reformers. Religious insight has again and again furnished the basis for such creative criticism of existing practices, and we shall do well to consider such bases of judgment as are provided in the religion of the Jewish-Christian tradition.

When most people think about the moral guidance that is afforded by religion the first thing to come to mind is the Ten Commandments and it is surprising how many of them regard these as the last word in moral requirement. The writer has had occasion to conduct repeatedly a series of open forum discussions in a training camp for high-school boys who had been selected for posts of leadership in Hi-Y clubs. They have been intelligent and alert boys who entered into the discussions in lively fashion. For purposes of stimulating their thought, and to get some indication as to where they were in their thinking on religious and moral questions, responses were secured from them to a religious opinion test which listed a series of statements to which they could check their reactions as true, false, or uncertain. One of these statements was, "The Ten Commandments are the highest moral law of the Christian." Out of 708 responses 93 per cent checked this statement as true, 4 per cent as false, and 3 per cent as uncertain. I have reason to believe that a cross section of adults would respond in about the same way.

It does not require prolonged consideration to prove that the Decalogue does not represent the highest moral law of the Christian. The highest moral imperatives cannot be expressed adequately in the terms of negative prohibitions and eight of the ten are so expressed. The two exceptions are, "Honor thy father and thy mother," and "Remember the Sabbath day to keep it holy," and the latter has been interpreted negatively as a prohibition against engaging in work on that day. Moreover, there are many recognized offenses against a Christian conscience that are not covered in any direct way by these injunctions. One has only to ask which of the Ten Commandments did the priest and the Levite in the parable of the Good Samaritan break? Or Dives, the rich man, in his neglect of Lazarus, the suffering beggar, at his gate? Or those who suffered condemnation in the parable of the Last Judgment?

What has happened is that the modern generation does not know the Ten Commandments; they simply know that there is such a decalogue which has come to symbolize in their minds the demands of Christian morality. In response to a questionnaire circulated among 152 students in freshman English sections of a midwestern university only three could name all ten of the commandments, the average number named being between five and six. This was borne out in the author's experience with the Hi-Y leaders mentioned above. When challenged to defend their estimate of the Decalogue, they would often quote in reply sayings of Jesus, such as the Golden Rule, or the Great Commandment, as if they were included in the Ten Commandments. For most people these commandments have become simply a conventionalized symbol of Christian ethics.

But deflate current misconceptions of this ancient code as we may, it remains a very important landmark in moral progress and its injunctions contain basic insights with which we can never dispense nor disregard except at great social peril. They do not express the highest Christian ideals, but men cannot play fast and loose with the Ten Commandments and be moral.

THE TEACHINGS OF JESUS

For Christians, for those who acknowledge Christ as the Lord of Life, the teachings of Jesus as given in precept and example constitute the highest moral authority. But it is important to ask just what kind of moral guidance Jesus gives. It is evident that he did not put forth a set of rules and regulations giving specific instructions as to how one ought to act in every particular situation that arises in connection with conduct. One finds no specific directive in the teachings of Jesus covering the question whether it is right or wrong to drink alcoholic beverage. Another problem that is very real in the lives of young people who are growing up that is covered by no specific teaching of Jesus is, "Under what circumstances is it right, and when is it wrong, for a boy to bestow a kiss upon a girl friend or for the girl to accept it?" One could build an imposing list of questions that involve moral decisions that are nowhere answered directly and specifically in the teachings of Jesus. The New Testament is not a rule book which furnishes ready-made answers to all perplexing questions with respect to right conduct. Instead of laying down rules Jesus taught some fundamental principles of conduct, the application of which to particular situations must be made by individuals and societies, and the process is not always an easy one.

One of these principles has become broadly known as the Golden Rule, "Whatsoever ye would that men should do to you, do ye even so to them." Most of the great moral teachers of the world have voiced this principle, at least in its negative form, and probably no principle has greater practical value in helping people to discover a proper course of action. But it may be questioned whether the Golden Rule can stand alone as a sufficient guide to conduct. Unless it is flanked by other moral principles which together form a constellation, it would appear that this one alone may be employed in support of inferior moral ends.

People who like to drink to the point of intoxication as a method of relaxation like to have their friends drink with them and invite them to do so. In turn they like to be invited to the drinking parties given by others. Here we have an application of the Golden Rule to a practice that is highly questionable. Even the Golden Rule of itself cannot be accepted as an infallible guide to conduct.

This danger is removed, however, when it is linked with others which Jesus also taught as fundamental, such as the sacredness and supreme worth of persons, that sincerity of motive is more important than outward conformity to law, that evil can be overcome only by positive goodness, that the measure of greatness is found in the value and extent of service to fellow men, and pre-eminently the Great Commandment: "Thou shalt love the Lord thy God with all thy heart, with all thy soul, and with all thy mind; and thou shalt love thy neighbor as thyself." That this double injunction drawn from two Old Testament writings was regarded by Jesus as the supreme law of life is evident from the comment that follows: "There is none other commandment greater than these." Here we seem to arrive at a final moral principle, which will ever call for widening application with the further development of life, but which will never be superseded.

Jesus roots his whole moral system in a religious conviction concerning the nature of God and his attitude toward men, namely, unfathomable love. The man who loves God as Jesus represented him as the ideal Father will have a high regard for himself as the object of God's love, and if he loves another as himself, he will not hold the other in low regard. All persons become sacred and of inestimable worth. In this connection it is of interest to note the words of a widely read modern moral theorist, Walter Lippmann, who affirms: "The politics, law, and morality of the Western World are an evolution from the religious conviction that all men are persons and that the human person is inviolable."[2] He too finds the basis of morality in the religious insight that persons are sacred and are not to be treated arbitrarily. The ultimate test of right and wrong is the effect of any action upon persons, on oneself, but equally upon others. Whatever makes for the highest well-being of people is right; whatever militates against the true welfare of people is wrong.

What does it mean to love your neighbor as yourself? Jesus is not

[2] *A Great Society.* Preface.

referring to any form of romantic love, nor is this a command to like people who do detestable things. He enjoins good will, a concern for your neighbor's good comparable to your concern for your own. This kind of love can be extended even to an enemy whose present actions you may deplore. The exercise of this kind of love works to bind all men together into a community of experience in which the welfare of each member becomes the common concern of all. Only as the Golden Rule is interpreted in the light of this imperative to love fellow men can it have its fullest and most positive meaning. Undergirded by the other moral principles of Jesus and supremely the Great Commandment it becomes the most useful of practical rules for the guidance of life.

SOME PRACTICAL TESTS

The task of making the application of moral principles to practical life as lived in a great variety of situations and circumstances is not always easy, and many times it will call for the exercise of the highest reason. In facing a difficult moral decision there are certain questions which may well be asked, and, if honestly answered, should enable one to make the right decision in most cases. The natural question to raise first is, what will be the effect of the proposed line of conduct on the person himself. Will it be degrading in its effect, or will it make for an increase of self-respect and the enrichment of his personal life? If it is determined that the result would be harmful to the person, one should judge the action as wrong without further ado, except in a possible case of self-sacrifice for the sake of some higher social good.

A second question would consider the effect upon others. Would it make for blessing or blight upon the lives of others affected? Would it add to their happiness or their woe? If the former, it may be presumed thus far to be right; if the latter, wrong. If this test is passed successfully, then that of time might be applied, namely, what will be the long-run effect of the contemplated action. An important aspect of every temptation experience is to yield to a seemingly imperious demand of an immediate good or satisfaction at the expense of a greater but more remote good. To sell out a greater good for a lesser one is the essence of sinful action.

A fourth test which might well be applied is that of publicity. When facing a decision whether or not to follow a particular course of action, it should be helpful to imagine what your reactions would be, if in case of an unexpected turn of events, the spotlight of publicity should be turned on your behavior in this situation and the same should be broadcast to the world through press and radio. Would you be proud of your action? Would you be embarrassed but unashamed; or would you be overcome by a sense of shame? A person might well be embarrassed by unexpected publicity of perfectly proper action, but if the reaction should be a feeling of shame the presumption would be that the contemplated action is wrong.

The test of universality is another to which a considered mode of behavior should be submitted. What would be the result if the mode of action under consideration should become the universal practice of people in like situations? A student may be under terrific pressure to pass a certain course of study for failure may mean that he will be dropped from college. By some clever cheating in an examination he is confident that he could secure the requisite mark, and he comes under strong temptation because he is very anxious to remain in college. He rationalizes the situation, reminding himself that he has a grudge against the teacher as he seems "to have it in" for him, and is rather incompetent anyhow, and the only way he can get a fair break for himself is to cheat. But suppose he asks himself, "What would be the result if every student under severe pressure, who thinks he has a grievance against the teacher, should resort to cheating?" He should see that there can be an advantage for the cheater only when most of the members of the class are honest. If all cheated, no one would be benefited and grade marks would be meaningless. Therefore, since he wants most people to be honest, even if he should cheat, his proposed conduct will not pass the test of universal adoption and should be adjudged wrong.

Even these tests may not be infallible, but contemplated action which can meet the tests of personal welfare, the good of others, of time, publicity and universal adoption will not miss the mark very far of good and wholesome conduct.

CHAPTER X

Prayer

NO EXPRESSION of religion is more universal than the practice of prayer. Every religion endorses it in some form, at least, and by many it is considered to be the very heart of the matter. Convictions among religious people concerning prayer do not divide them into contending schools of thought. People do not all think alike concerning the subject, but the divisions are not so much between theories that are in opposition to each other, as between naïve and mature views, or between primitive and intelligent conceptions. There are low forms and high forms of prayer.

It is not always easy to distinguish prayer from other attitudes and psychological states, that obviously are closely related. For example, let us suppose a person is vacationing at the seashore, where it is possible to watch the summer sun set, as it were, into the sea. In a perfectly relaxed state he gives himself up fully to the enjoyment of the setting sun and is enraptured by the changing shades of color as they play upon banks of clouds and clothe the sky in indescribable glory. He is aware of a great exultation within his inner spirit as he senses the grandeur that invests the universe, and his heart is filled with gratitude for the privilege of experiencing beauty in so exalted a form. Is such an attitude prayer?

Let us think again of a person enjoying a state of perfect relaxation and repose who gives himself to reverie, letting his thoughts go where they will without any effort to determine their direction. He continues in a highly receptive mood, his mind quite open to suggestion or inspiration from without. May such an act be prayer? Or picture a situation which calls for an act of meditation with respect to some serious problem which troubles one, the solution of which is difficult. The subject carries on a mental conversation within himself as he takes account of all the factors, and weighs the possible alternatives of action. He is definitely seeking light on the best course to pursue in the situation. Is this prayer?

A brilliant student leader, who made no religious professions, once told the writer that it was his habit to spend a few minutes before retiring each night checking over the events of that day, appraising his successes and failures, endeavoring to see how he might have improved his course of action, and in the light of these revelations to determine his program and make his resolutions for the next day. He wanted to know whether or not he was engaging in prayer.

We may also conceive of a person who entertains some great longing in his heart and mind. Again and again he concentrates his thoughts upon this dominant desire of his life. He wishes with all his being for the consummation of his great desire. Is such concentration upon a deep-seated longing prayer? Or consider the case of one who comes under the spell of a great challenge to enlist in the warfare against some flagrant evil that corrupts society, and solemnly vows to enter the struggle with all his power. Young Lincoln, on a trip to New Orleans, was so moved by the cruelty of what he saw at a slave auction that he was moved to declare, "If ever I get the chance to strike that thing, I shall hit it with all my might." Are we praying when we make a solemn vow?

In answer to these questions it may be affirmed that any one of these experiences may, or may not, be prayer. Prayer finds expression in a variety of forms and moods and the above cases are illustrations of some of the more important of these. The distinguishing characteristic, however, is not the form, but the objective reference. Prayer is communion with God. Prayer takes place whenever a person becomes aware of the presence of God in such a way that he senses a converse between himself and the Divine.

The person lost in the rapture of a glorious sunset may be led almost unconsciously into an act of prayer if the scene suggests to him the immediacy of God's presence. The person giving himself to reverie may be engaged in prayer, if he is listening for the voice of God and is keeping himself sensitive to divine guidance. Probably no aspect of prayer is in greater need of cultivation than the listening or receptive phase. As Muriel Lester says, "Prayer is not asking for things, but a quiet concentration of the mind, 'held still and serene' in the presence of God, so that something of His wisdom, His power, and His patience can permeate one's very being." The student engaged in life-appraisal is praying if his passing-in-review of the day's activities is done for the purpose of throwing the light of God upon his outward acts and inner attitudes. William Adams Brown has said of prayer, "It is not the saying of words to God, but letting the mind rove over the range of human experience as it is illuminated by the thought of God, taking up one by one the familiar events and experiences of daily life—the persons one knows, the responsibility one faces, the sorrows one has to bear— as they are transformed by the new context in which they are put by the purpose of God."[1] Meditation is a form of prayer when it is a means of determining the course of action God would approve, and concentration upon a wish may be prayer if the co-operation of God is sought in its fulfillment. Likewise, the taking of a vow is prayer, when it is a means of consecrating oneself before God to work with him for the attainment of a righteous end. In the words of E. Herman, prayer "is the highest and most dynamic form of interaction between the human and the Divine. It is the whole personality—intellect as well as emotion and will—energising in fellowship with the Lord of all Life."[2]

PRAYER OBJECTIVES

In addition to taking a variety of forms prayer may be directed to a number of different ends. When classified according to the ends sought, prayer may be divided into the following kinds: thanksgiving, confession, petition, intercession, communion, and consecration. Little comment is necessary to make clear the nature of each of these types. Thanksgiving is, of course, a response of gratitude to God as the source of all good gifts for the blessings of life. The prayer of confession is an acknowledgment of failures and shortcomings to the end that the penitent may be forgiven and restored to a state of divine favor. Petition represents man's effort to put himself into alliance with higher powers than his own that will help him fulfill his quest for the necessities and

[1] *The Life of Prayer in a World of Science,* p. 51.
[2] *Creative Prayer,* p. 32.

goods of life and accord him moral deliverance over the temptations of evil. In intercession the man of prayer seeks not his own but another's good. In communion the person praying seeks God, not for what he can give, but for what he is. The child may think of his parents largely in terms of what they can do for him. But as he becomes more mature in his appreciations, he comes to value them more for what they are and seeks no greater favor than the blessing of intimate fellowship with them. So in the prayer of communion one seeks no other good than that of fellowship with God. In the prayer of consecration one dedicates himself and his own powers to the service of God in the pursuit of high ends and noble causes.

OBSTACLES TO THE PRACTICE OF PRAYER

In the present age prayer to a great extent has gone out of fashion. This generation does not sense the need for prayer that has characterizd those of the past. It is not altogether easy to account for the change, but one of the most important factors is man's increasing control over the material conditions of his life. With the development of the processes of production to the point of abundant provision of the elemental necessities of life, and with the increase of social control over the distribution of these necessities, man has greatly heightened his sense of security in the physical world. With respect to the need for food, clothing, shelter, and protection from the ravages of disease man is not confronted with anything like as many awful specters and terrible uncertainties as were his forefathers. Having learned how, through cooperation and the application of scientific knowledge, to appropriate the earth's resources, he no longer feels the need of direct aid from the gods in this sphere. This decreased sense of immediate dependence upon the favor of higher powers has operated against resort to prayer as a means of propitiating higher powers upon whom man believed himself directly dependent for the fulfillment of the basic needs of life.

A second obstacle to the continuance of the practice of prayer is the great stress that a scientific age places on the reign of law throughout the universe. As long as men conceived of God not only as superior to, but as in no way bound by the laws of nature, there was every justification for appealing to this transcendent power to grant things which appeared impossible of accomplishment through natural means. But when God is thought of as immanent within the processes of nature, and as never acting contrary to the laws of the natural order, then it becomes folly to ask him to set aside that order for the benefit of some individual; and it becomes difficult to perceive just how prayer can make any difference in the working out of the natural course of events. In other words, it is difficult to understand how prayer can operate as an important casual factor in a natural order operating under a system of law.

Sometimes even religious convictions are used as an argument against prayer. It is held that an all-wise and an all-knowing God knows our needs without our asking. He is more aware of our real needs than we ourselves. If he is as good as the Bible maintains when it declares that he is more anxious to bestow good gifts upon men than are earthly parents to give good things to their children, then prayer should be unnecessary. It is needed neither to inform God of our needs, nor to awaken in him the impulse to generosity. Why then should it be necessary for man to pray?

Another objection to prayer comes from the psychologists who, because they cannot catch God in their net of psychological analysis, declare that prayer is simply a form of self-deception rather than actual converse with an objective reality. They may be generous enough to admit that as a form of auto-suggestion it may have real value in integrating the life and heightening the powers of him who prays, but they still insist that a person's prayers do not get beyond himself. Let a person become convinced, however, that he cannot contact God through prayer and he will soon cease the pretense of prayer despite the acknowledgment of its critics that it may have salutary effects.

A practical difficulty that many face in their efforts to cultivate an effective prayer life is the experience of unanswered prayer. They may have poured out their hearts in earnest appeal for some deep desire which has never been fulfilled, or they may have put their whole souls into the expression of some inner longing, and experienced only disappointment and frustration. After such experience it is not surprising that they conclude that prayer is unavailing.

FACING THE DIFFICULTIES

Advocates of prayer in the modern age declare that these objections rest upon false ideas of the true nature of prayer and of God's working in the world. Prayer has gone through an evolution in the experience of men and the difficulties arise because many people continue to think of it in the light of an outgrown stage in its development. Primitive man incorporated a good deal of magic in his attempts at prayer. Through the use of potent formulæ, or with the help of powerful fetishes, he endeavored to force his will upon the world and to coerce higher powers to grant his wishes. With increasing insight into the nature of life and his relative place in the world, he saw the folly of trying to force his will upon the gods. He then turned to propitiation of the higher powers and endeavored by means of persuasion to induce them to grant his requests. Prayer became a form of begging, through which man hoped to overcome the reluctance of the gods to the end that they would grant favors which they had not intended to bestow. The concept of prayer entertained by many people today has not gotten beyond this point. In the light of this conception it does appear to be folly to beseech an all-wise and completely good and generous God to grant men's requests for things which his greater wisdom has not ordained as for the best. Prayer then is simply a means of inducing God to become indulgent.

A new conception of prayer is arising, however, which sees it not as a means of persuading God to change his mind, but as a method by which man may bring his mind into fuller accord with the divine will to the end of co-operating with God in the carrying forward of his designs in the world. Prayer is not a means of securing God's co-operation in the fulfillment of human wishes, but a way of furthering human co-operation in the realization of God's purposes. This type of prayer is well illustrated in the prayers of Jesus. Consider the prayer he gave to his disciples as an example of effective praying. The primary petition of the Lord's prayer is, "*Thy* Kingdom come; *Thy* will be done on earth as it is in heaven." Likewise, in the prayer of the Garden of Gethsemane, when Jesus poured out his earnest desire that the cup of bitterness might be taken from him, in each instance he qualified his request with the deeper one, "Nevertheless, not my will but thine be done." Prayer was the means by which Jesus sought to bring his own innermost longings into accord with the higher purposes of God. Such prayer is believed to be a high form of co-operation with God.

The question may still be raised, however, how prayer may make any real difference in the course of events even when so conceived? We must proceed largely with the help of analogy. It is evident within the human realm of action that there is much more likelihood of something coming to pass when two people are united in their purpose to achieve a desirable end than if one alone desires it. The more people who join in desiring a given end, the greater the probability of its being realized. Likewise, it would appear that there is greater likelihood of some desirable end being achieved when a man becomes united with God in the earnest desire for the achievement of some righteous goal, than when God alone desires it. Conceivably some things may become possible when God and man become united in purpose, that are not possible to God without human co-operation. As men become more united with God in the purpose to see his will achieved in human society, the more that end becomes possible. Prayer then becomes a means of harmonizing human desires with divine desires, and human wills with the divine purpose, to the end of making things possible that would not be possible if men did not pray. As Professor Wieman puts it, "Prayer is adjusting the personality to God in such a way that God can work more potently for good than he otherwise could, as the outstretched wings of a bird enable the rising currents to carry it to higher levels." So conceived, prayer must not be resorted to as a substitute for other necessary forms of co-operation with God, such as the exercise of intelligence, or the application of human energies, but should be an important supplement to the use of intelligence and human effort. Thus it may be a very vital form of human co-operation with the divine program. This is a most reasonable assumption, if God can function best in society through persons who are committed to his purposes.

What now of the objection that prayer would violate the reign of law in the world? As here described prayer no more violates the natural order than do two friends who engage in intimate converse for the sake of attaining a better understanding of each other or a higher degree of mutuality in their living. In the words of Dr. Fosdick, "The law of friendship is communion, and prayer is the fulfilling of the law."

The objection that prayer is unnecessary because of the great generosity of God, likewise falls to the ground under a more enlightened view of prayer. From the higher view prayer ceases to be regarded as a means of persuading God to bestow gifts upon men, but is viewed rather as a necessary factor in releasing his abundant generosity. In the classic phrase of Archbishop Trench, prayer is not "an overcoming of God's reluctance, but a laying hold of God's highest willingness." It is a form of co-operation through which man helps to make God's amazing goodness manifest.

To the psychologist's objection that prayer is but a form of self-deception, it may be answered that in converse between two humans it is doubtful if psychology by directing attention only to what takes place in the brain and nervous system of one member of the conversation could establish the fact of a second party in the proceeding without the aid of sight and sound. That which would be observed in such a case would resemble the effects of meditation, or converse with oneself. If psychology cannot without the aid of sight and sound, which are aspects of the science of physics, establish the fact of a conversation being carried on between two people, how much less competent is it to determine whether a person converses with that which is objective to himself in prayer where the object belongs to the realm of the invisible, and where the aids from the science of physics are not applicable. The place, moreover, at which God conceivably contacts man is at the point of his own best thoughts, insights and inspirations. The experience is that of reinforcement of one's own best. The contact is not like a telegraphic connection with a deity far-removed, but represents an opening of the heart and mind to God who is already there seeking fuller entrance. Psychology assumes too much when it asserts that in prayer one does not contact that which is above and beyond oneself, although it may be impossible to distinguish where the self ends and that which is not self begins.

The principal reply to be made by defenders of prayer to the objection of unanswered prayers is that usually such prayers ask amiss. They represent efforts to bend God's will to man's, not man's to God. Let man pray as Jesus did, "Nevertheless not my will but thine be done," and he will not pray in vain. The cup was not removed for Jesus. He had to drink it to the dregs, but he went from the Garden of Gethsemane with clarified vision of the divine will for his life, new determination to see it through, new moral courage and recovered poise. His prayer was abundantly answered, not as he at first desired, but in ways more significant and meaningful than he had conceived. There will always be difficult questions concerning what constitutes proper subjects and legitimate requests to be included in prayer, but the advocates of prayer maintain that God is always responsive to every sincere approach to himself, if the one who prays does not endeavor to dictate the mode of the answer.

From the testimony of those who have gained proficiency in the art of prayer it is possible to set forth a number of conditions which are essential to effective praying. The teachings of Jesus declare a number of these. One of the first precepts to be emphasized by him was the necessity of freeing the mind of all distractions. In accord with oriental love of figurative language he advised men when they pray to enter their closets and close the door and pray to the Father in secret. What Jesus meant to emphasize was the importance of putting oneself in a situation where it was possible to give attention completely and without interruption to the business of prayer. For this purpose it was his own custom to seek the solitude of the mountain side under the cover of the darkness of night. Some people have acquired the art of an inner solitude even in the midst of people and much activity. When riding in trains, street cars or busses, they are able to shut everything else out of the focus of attention and give themselves fully to communion with God. Such an achievement is the product of much discipline of self, and for the novice the best procedure is to seek actual physical solitude where it is a simple matter to shut out from attention all extraneous matters.

A second requirement for effective praying is that it be engaged in against a background of high thinking. "As a man thinketh in his heart, so is he" and if through prayer he would establish a greater unity with God, his prayers must be supported by his thoughts. One cannot habitually think mean thoughts and successfully offer prayers of noble aspiration. On this point some observations of Dr. Harry Emerson Fosdick are particularly helpful. He cites a passage from Apostle Paul's letter to the Philippians:

In nothing be anxious; but in everything by prayer and supplication with thanksgiving let your requests be made known unto God. And the peace of God, which passeth all understanding, shall guard your hearts and your thoughts in Christ Jesus. Finally, brethren, whatsoever things are true, whatsoever things are honorable, whatsoever things are just, whatsoever things are pure, whatsoever things are lovely, whatsoever things are of good report; if there be any virtue, and if there be any praise, think on these things.— Phil. 4:6–8.

There follows this comment:

This connection of verses on great praying and right thinking is not accidental. A man cannot habitually indulge in mean, perverse, or abominable thoughts and suddenly come out of them into unimpeded communion with God. An automobile can be shifted from "low" to "high" with a stroke of the hand, but not so a man's mind. Real praying costs *habitual self-discipline in thinking*—the pure in heart see God.[3]

If it is not fitting to rush pell-mell into the presence of an earthly sovereign, how much less to approach God in this manner. The approach must be in a reverent attitude and this calls for a preparation of mind for which high thinking is an important essential.

Regularity with respect to time and place is conducive to successful achievement in the art of praying. It is possible, of course, to engage in prayer in any place at any time. But to have a place which the mind associates with the practice of communion with God and to have a time when one habitually turns to prayer as naturally as he thinks of luncheon at noon will greatly aid in building an effectual prayer habit. Some there are who have graduated from reliance upon fixed times and places inasmuch as the attitude of communion has itself become habitual, so that frequently and naturally in the course of every day they turn to God in prayer. Such a disposition is not acquired quickly, however, but represents the fruition of years of discipline in which regularity is an important factor.

Another point which Jesus emphasized in his teaching concerning prayer was the necessity of exercising one's faith in the efficacy of prayer: "Therefore I say unto you, all things whatsoever ye pray and ask for, believe that ye receive them, and ye shall have them." (Mark 11:24.) It is essential to pray in a spirit of expectancy. It may be well to assert again that all prayer should be directed to the end of bringing

[3] Fosdick: *The Meaning of Prayer*, p. 72.

God's will to pass in the world. But if the one praying is persuaded that the specific object of prayer meets this primary condition, he then should pray with assurance that his prayer will make a difference and produce results. The first result should occur in the life of him who prays. Professor H. N. Wieman asserts: "When God answers prayer he transforms persons, institutions and ideals into a higher unity of richer value. He who prays must be the first one to undergo this transformation. He initiates it by his prayer."

Turning again to Jesus, perseverance is indicated as one of the requisites of successful praying. Prayer is not always easy. There are rare experiences of spiritual exaltation, more frequent for some than others, when prayer is the spontaneous response of the human spirit. Over against these are many commonplace hours when one prays only with great difficulty. In such times prayer may seem unreal, and it is difficult to bring oneself into the right mood or to effect the proper degree of concentration. Persistence is required to overcome the deadening effect of these seemingly unfruitful periods and to make prayer avail.

Most important of all conditions of effective prayer is sincerity. There must be a high degree of correspondence between one's innermost thoughts and desires and that which is expressed in prayer. When men pray outwardly as they know they ought to pray, but inwardly desire something else, prayer is of no avail. To be sure a person may recognize the presence in his life of habits, desires and attitudes which ought not to be there and which his best judgment condemns and may earnestly pray for help in exorcising these things. When the desire to rid self of evil propensities is sincere, then prayer is justified no matter how deeply entrenched the wrong, but one cannot pray as St. Augustine confessed he did in his unregenerate state, "O, Lord, make me pure, but not yet."

Sincerity in prayer involves a willingness to share the cost involved in the granting of the prayer. If one prays for the relief of the poor, and expects his prayer to make a difference, he cannot continue to live in personal comfort and fail to share his own ample resources with the needy. If he prays that the light of the gospel be carried to those who dwell in darkness, he must be willing to carry his full part in supporting the missionary enterprise by contribution and service at the home base. If a student prays for wisdom, he must be willing to pay the cost of devotion to his studies. The advocate of international peace who prays for peace among the nations, must demonstrate his sincerity by his active devotion to the program of peace action and to the cause of building the requisite institutions of peace. Prayer to be real must correspond with the purposes and desires that dominate a person's character and life. Such prayer is always effective in the direction of its ends, like hunger and thirst in their realm. When prayer is wholly sincere, its effectiveness may be beyond measure.

CHAPTER XI

The Case for Immortality

A SUBJECT which will always provoke discussion if introduced into group conversation is that of immortality. One reason, perhaps, why it lends itself so readily to lively discussion is that in dealing with it one must resort largely to pure speculation, as the amount of verifiable evidence that can be advanced in favor of the belief is extremely little, except for limited aspects of the problem. Whatever reasoning is done must proceed largely by deduction from certain broad generalizations or general beliefs, rather than by induction from a body of accumulated idea. This does not deter people, however, from discussing the matter with avidity.

How much importance should be attached to the subject is difficult to determine. Certainly it has been overemphasized when declared to be the chief concern of man's present life, overshadowing all other problems, and when religion's only purpose is to insure man of a blessed experience in the beyond. On the other hand it is equally fallacious to take the attitude that it does not matter and assume complete indifference. A man's present life is certainly to be tempered in some way by his conception of death and of what lies beyond.

FOUR CONCEPTIONS

Various ideas of the state of existence after death are prevalent among peoples of different cultural groups and backgrounds. Confining our attention to ideas in the Occidental world we find that they fall into four categories, the biological, social, impersonal, and personal conceptions. By biological immortality is meant that continuing stream of life of which living individuals are simply the contemporary expressions. The continuing element is within the protoplasm and more particularly the chromosomes and genes. In these latter elements are found the factors which determine the relative fixity of species and the personal traits which are handed down from generation to generation. These qualities are passed along, in combination with other qualities that result from the union of different streams, in an unbroken line so long as the process of reproduction proceeds without interruption. "Individuals," says one geneticist, "become mere incidents in the scheme of life; mere rocks and banks which confine the stream yet without which the stream would not exist." A particular individual inherits all that he possesses from those who have preceded him and passes on all that he is to those who succeed him. The specific influence of that particular individual upon his successors diminishes with succeeding generations as the chromosomes of each new conception represent a mixture with those of another line so that after a few generations the traits of this particular ancestor represent a small element of the total biological inheritance. On the other hand, presumably the number of one's descendants may increase or even multiply in succeeding generations so that what is lost by reason of the diminishing influence of a particular ancestor may be compensated by the increasing number of individuals in whom the strain is represented. In a normal case the number of descendants should be in inverse proportion to the degree of his determination of inherited traits in his successors of any particular generation. If one's particular line expires, that individual would forfeit immortality, and no person will attain a higher degree of immortality than that which belongs to the human race as a particular species.

There is truth in the social view of immortality for those who recognize the nature of our social heritage. This view maintains that the influence of one man's life reaches out and affects society about him. In the case of great leaders it is quite obvious that the world is forever different by reason of what they did and said. In the case of the greatest of these they have attained an immortality in the memories of men. Names like Moses, Plato, Augustine, Luther, George Washington, Abraham Lincoln, Napoleon, Alexander the Great, Julius Cæsar, and so on through a long list, will ever be remembered as well as the accomplishments for which they are noted. In a lesser degree every person that lives leaves his imprint on the texture of life, and though his contribution is unrecognized and unremembered the total pattern is different from what it would have been if he had not lived. In the permanent contribution that is possible for every life to make to the social heritage of the race, one may gain some measure of immortality. Such immortality is likewise limited, however, by the limitations that adhere to the race itself.

The impersonal view of immortality is capable of varied expression. It may assume the existence of a superior spirit or world soul from which all individual souls take their rise. In event of death the individual soul is reabsorbed into the great spirit from which it came but retains none of its individuality.

One current conception of impersonal immortality conceives of life as a great reality independent of matter but which uses matter as an instrument of its purposes. When the right conditions are established, life may enter into a combination with matter and the result is a living organism. Small increments of life become individualized in persons, and through the activities, acquired skills and appreciations of these persons the individualized portions of life are enriched. At death the temporary association of an increment of life with matter is dissolved and the life is reabsorbed into the great central reservoir from which it emerged, but carries back with it whatever richness it may have acquired in the individual state. Hence, by the contributions of an untold number of individuals, the sum total of life continues to grow in richness and each succeeding generation will have the advantage of a measure of life potentially richer than that which belonged to its predecessors. Through the enrichment which the individual is able to make to the great ocean of life, he attains his immortality. An excellent summary of this mode of thought has been written by C. E. M. Joad:

Just as the modern theory of physics envisages a common source of radioactive energy from which each atom of energy emanates, and to which, conceivably, it returns, so, it is suggested, each unit of vital energy, which when associated with matter, we call a living organism, reverts at the breakup of the body to a main stream or reservoir of life, enriched by the skill and knowledge, the more consciousness and the enlarged power of understanding which the individual has acquired throughout a lifetime of effort and struggle, and with these enriches in its turn the life stream from which it took its rise. If living organisms are to be regarded as life's contrivances for facilitating the process of its own evolution, it is clear that their struggles and their victories, their acquisitions of skill and of knowledge, the sharpening of their faculties and the heightening of their powers— all the changes, in short, that happen to them in their lives—are not matters of indifference to life as a whole, but have a direct bearing upon its present status and future prospects. And the conclusion which this view of creative evolution suggests is that life as a whole is constantly being fertilised and developed by the acquisitions of knowledge, skill, and insight which its individual units make for it, and appears in consequence in each successive objectification of itself in matter at a slightly higher level. It is suggested, that is to say, not so much that I am the richer in vital endowment because of the efforts of my particular ancestors, though this may in some measure be true, but rather that the generation to which I belong enjoys life as a whole at a higher level and of a richer quality because of the acquisitions of all the preceding generations.[1]

The accepted Christian position with respect to life after death has been the doctrine of personal individual immortality which affirms the continuance of the self with its individual characteristics beyond the incident of physical death. This continuance may be conceived in immaterial terms apart from the body, or in connection with a resurrected body, or as held by the Apostle Paul, in a new or heavenly body. The balance of the chapter will be devoted to considerations bearing upon the prospect of personal immortality.

IS PERSONAL IMMORTALITY DESIRABLE?

One question that needs to be faced early in the consideration is the question whether or not personal immortality is desirable. If it should be concluded that it is not to be desired, there would be no need to go further, for in view of the lack of evidence to support it, a person convinced of its undesirability would refuse to believe in it and would be uninterested in arguments that might be marshaled in support of it. If the question is rephrased so as to ask what would be the nature of a life after death that would be everlastingly desirable, it is not easy to formulate a satisfying answer. Traditional conceptions of the city with golden streets and pearly gates evoke little interest in the modern mind.

[1] *Guide to Modern Thought*, pp. 151–152.

The prospect of singing in heavenly choruses or of playing harps in a celestial symphony might be an inviting prospect for a limited time but would pall as an eternal activity. Likewise one could look forward to a period of blissful and undisturbed rest, after a life of trying and discouraging labor on earth; but the prospect of a rest which never ends and is never disturbed by any thrilling events is not especially inviting. The restless spirit of the modern man refuses to be satisfied with any heaven that represents a static condition, no matter how inviting and blissful it might be for a limited period.

What man has always done in forming his pictures of a heavenly existence is to project into it the complete fulfillment of the highest desires that he knows in his earthly experience. The Indian who could imagine nothing more desirable and thrilling than successful hunting thought of the after-life as the happy hunting ground. Early Christian victims of Imperial Roman persecutions who languished in vermin-infested dungeons conceived of heaven as a place of cleanliness and light, where they should know the joy of clean white linen garments. The Mohammedan soldier who risked all the comforts of family and home and accepted the rigors of war as the champion of the faith of Allah anticipated as a reward the pleasure of reclining upon soft couches in cool arbors where blue-eyed maidens would serve delectable wines, the quaffing of which would be delightful in the immediate experience and would be succeeded by no undesirable aftermaths. Through this process of projection of desire, many pictures have been drawn of heavenly bliss, but most of them lose their fascination when one asks himself if he would like to indulge in such activity eternally.

The case for a desirable after-life is not altogether hopeless, however, nor is it necessary to depart from the accepted method of determining what would be desirable. One of the lessons which mankind has learned is that the human spirit cannot long remain satisfied in any one particular state. One of the elements that makes life continually interesting is the factor of change, and particularly development in the course of which life continues to open up new possibilities and to challenge one with the prospect of new and higher attainments. Life fascinates only so long as one feels the lure of some new goal or achievement ahead. "To live," says Rabbi A. H. Silver, "is to feel continuously the teem and thrust of expanding life within one's soul, the thrill of new ideas, the throb of new purposes, the stir of revelation and new insight." Since it is the constant opportunity for continued growth and development that causes the present life to retain its interest, a heavenly existence to appeal to dynamic moderns must offer similar possibilities. If the life beyond the grave can be pictured as one in which the human spirit freed from the limitations of its physical embodiment can continue to grow and develop, unfold new possibilities, and enter into successively new and higher appreciations without limit, it becomes something to be much desired by anyone who has learned to love life. The prospect of going on from achievement to achievement, of broadening the scope of one's experience, of enlarging the significance of one's service to the Kingdom of God, and of enriching the circle of worth-while fellowship would be an intriguing challenge. Although we may not be able to fill in the detail of such a program, it is possible on the basis of this outline to conceive of a type of personal immortality which is highly desirable.

OBSTACLES TO BELIEF

Having determined that there is a conception of immortality which makes it desirable, we shall do well to turn our attention to the question to its possibility. Let us consider first arguments that are unfavorable to the belief. One such consideration urged against it is the difficulty we encounter when we endeavor to conceive its nature. Attention has already been directed to this obstacle. It will have to be admitted that the conditions under which man's soul continues to live after the death of the body are so different from those which prevail in his present experience that it becomes impossible to fill out the detailed specifications of the life to come. The fact that our sight is limited to the present existence is no real argument, however, against the possibility of continuance of life as will be shown more fully in connection with the constructive argument.

The fact that it has not been proven is also advanced as an argument against belief. It is true that no one has been able to demonstrate the fact of continued life of individual persons beyond death. Researchers in this and allied fields have come upon some startling phenomena for which no one can offer an adequate explanation and which may have some bearing on the matter, but as yet these have fallen short of demonstration of the truth of continuing existence. The argument from inability to demonstrate would have weight if it were possible to submit proof of the opposite. It is no more possible to prove the annihilation of the person in death than his continuance after death. This fact neutralizes the force of this contention.

The most serious difficulty to be overcome grows out of the relationship of the immaterial qualities of man's life to his physical organism, inasmuch as those characteristics which are held to persist beyond death are the qualities of mind. The question boils down to the nature of relationship which exists between the mind and the brain. Does mind represent the creation of the brain or is the brain the instrument through which the mind expresses itself in the physical order? According to the first view mind is the product of the brain even as light is the product of the burning of the candle. Snuff out the candle and there is no more light; destroy the brain and there is no mind. But it is also possible to think of the relationship under the analogy of a musical instrument. Music, to be sure, may be regarded as the function of the piano, but the piano does not create the music. The music is created in the mind of the composer. A piano is simply the instrument through which the composer brings his music to expression and transmits it for the appreciation of others. The piano may be destroyed but it will still be possible for the composer to find other ways of bringing his music to expression. Now if the brain is the instrument which the mind plays upon and through which it expresses itself in this physical order, it is conceivable that the mind is not dependent upon the brain for its existence, and may find other means of expression in another order different from this physical world which we now inhabit.

Those who hold the mind to be the product of the brain point in support of their position to the recently discovered facts about glandular functioning and show how by creating certain deficiencies in glandular secretions the working of the mind is affected, and conversely how by correcting such deficiencies when they occur better mental functioning at once becomes evident. The supporters of the instrumental theory of the brain, on the other hand, direct attention to what the science of psychiatry has revealed about the power of the mind to affect bodily conditions. Many bodily disorders are being traced directly to mental complexes, and the resolving of the complexes results in the correction of the physical disorders and the disappearance of alarming symptoms. The issue still hangs in the balance. If the conclusion is established that the brain produces the mind, it would seem to deny the possibility of personal immortality. If the instrumental theory of the brain is accepted, the situation would be highly favorable to belief in immortality.

IN FAVOR OF BELIEF

Several of the arguments that are advanced in favor of belief in immortality rest for their validity upon the truth of certain assumptions about the nature of the world which are themselves not yet proven. This fact indicates how speculative is the nature of this belief. One such argument declares that immortality is necessary for the fulfillment of justice. The assumption is that justice is one of the inherent characteristics of the structure of our world. Justice in the lives of individual men, however, is constantly meeting defeat if death ends all. No sane person would hold that every person receives complete justice within the limits of his earthly life or that everyone receives the goods and ills of life strictly in accord with his deserts. If, therefore, justice is defeated in the present life, it requires a future life in which to fulfill itself, or the conclusion must be drawn that justice is not an essential characteristic of the nature of the world. Those who refuse to believe this find immortality necessary in order that the arc of justice may be completed.

The second argument, also based upon a great assumption, may be stated simply in this proposition: persons are too valuable to be destroyed. The assumption here is that our universe is rational. In the physical order the law of conservation is quite apparent. Matter may change its form but it cannot be destroyed in the sense of being annihilated. Solids may be changed to liquids, liquids to gases, and gases back into solids, but in the process there is no diminution of the total bulk of the matter. Viewing the same truth from a different angle, energies may be transformed from chemical to electrical to mechanical and vice versa, but in the changes there is no diminution in the total sum of energy. In a universe where conservation is so apparent in the physical world, is it reasonable to suppose that life is utterly indifferent to the fate of its finest products? Is that world rational which preserves physical energies and is indifferent to spiritual values which are achieved only in persons? But it would seem that just this is so if the greatest of human spirits are connected with life only by a thin gossamer thread which may be severed by an unfortunate accident to the body. In the words of Professor Montague, this places "the things we care for most at the mercy of those things we care for least." One may be driven to believe that conclusion, but if so, he will find it hard to believe at the same time in the reasonableness of the universe.

The full force of the above argument does not come home to one who thinks only in terms of his own immortality. Allowance must be made in this investigation as in others for the personal equation and the best way to make this provision is to consider it in relation to some-one else. Most of us could contemplate with equanimity the prospect of our own non-existence, but the whole question assumes a different aspect when we contemplate the annihilation of a soul who is more dear to us than our own souls. John Baillie suggests that we ought to think of this prospect in terms of the soul most precious to us.

One cannot contemplate without resentment a universe, which because of the failure of a body to function, no longer has a place in it for one's mother, or wife, or sweetheart. A world indifferent to spiritual values incarnate in human souls is an irrational world. This terrible thing may be true. But it is noteworthy that science in its realm proceeds on the unproven assumption of the rationality of the universe and is scoring remarkable successes in revealing the nature of relationships which exist in the world of physical matter and energy. May not equally great results emerge from interpreting the universe as rational in the realm of spiritual forces and relationships? If so, the intuition which persists that the world does not exclude from its life the spirits of our mothers and fathers, our sons and daughters, our friends and loved ones is well-founded.

An argument which has something more of an empirical basis is that which declares that the human soul is characterized by greater possibilities than can possibly be brought to expression in the brief span of our earthly existence. Simply stated, we seem to be made for a greater and fuller life than we here experience. Normal people do not exhaust the possibilities inherent in them in three score years and ten nor even in fourscore years. Every alert person is aware of desires in himself

which will never be fulfilled and interests which will never be cultivated to their full development and satisfaction. There are people with
literary aptitudes who never find opportunity to give these adequate
expression. There are people with latent musical abilities who never
have the opportunity to cultivate these and enrich the lives of themselves and others by reason of them. There are men with inventive
genius whose lives might be comparable to that of Thomas Edison for
their contributions to applied science, whose talent has remained buried
because of lack of educational opportunity. One of the things which
amazes those who are keen observers of life is the inexhaustible possibilities latent within human beings. As striking as has been the growth
and development of many people no intelligent person would claim
that human possibilities can find complete fulfillment in the present
order of life. We seem to be made for something greater for which this
life is a preparation and a partial anticipation. The human spirit demands something more for its own fulfillment.

We have admitted that appearances are against persistence of the
self. But we may raise the question as to which is the truer intimation,
appearances, or the presence of these evidences which indicate that man
is created for something greater than he can attain in the present world.
As Dr. Fosdick has pointed out in one of his inimitable analogies,[2] in
the case of an unborn babe in its mother's womb, if it could take account of appearances, birth would appear to be that crisis which would
mean death rather than the emergence into a fuller life. The appearances would be utterly misleading. But if account should be taken of
the meaning of all the developments that have taken place within the
human matrix the plain inference would be that something greater is
intended than can possibly be realized in the existing environment.
Therefore, the crisis of birth which appears like death, would in reality
portend an experience of emancipation into that large realm in which
these elaborate preparations will find their justification. Even so, the
event of physical death may be another stage in an emancipating process through which the human spirit finds opportunity to come into
its own. Such a conclusion would seem to accord very well with the
whole trend of the evolutionary process unless it be proven that this

[2] *As I See Religion*, p. 58 f.

process has arrived at a dead end in man as a physical being whose spiritual qualities are no more than the ephemeral relations of an intricate organization of matter.

Before concluding the survey of favorable arguments some attention should be given to certain religious arguments. The primary religious argument finds its basis in the faith of religious persons in the love and benevolence of God. The existence of a righteous and generous God who is deeply concerned for the welfare of individual persons is another unproved assumption despite its importance for the Christian religion. It is a faith, however, which seems to be amply justified and as such is the very core of the Christian system. In the light of this central faith, if personal immortality represents a benefit which men should desire, its denial would represent the denial either of God's goodness, or of his power. To refuse to grant the boon would be contrary to the dictates of love; to be unable to would be so severe a limitation on God's power as to disturb seriously man's confidence in his ability to determine the outcome of life. Either conclusion would be inconsistent with the accepted Christian conception of the nature of God. For those who find sufficient reason to accept the Christian idea of God as essentially true, the conclusion is justified that the power of God is pledged to the fulfillment of personal immortality if it is found to be desirable.

A further element of the religious approach holds that an assurance of immortality is found in the experience of Jesus in his triumph over death as certified by the apostles and recorded in the New Testament. For a Christian believer this argument has weight, even though he recognizes certain difficulties in connection with the record. Five accounts of the resurrection of Jesus can be found in the New Testament, that of the Apostle Paul in I Corinthians XV, and one in each of the Gospels. In matters of detail they are at hopeless variance. But one thing is clear, namely, that the same disciples who fled from fright at the time of Jesus' arrest, a few weeks later were preaching the crucified Jesus as the Messiah with a boldness that caused them to fear no authority or threat. The only logical way of accounting for this marvelous transformation is their own explanation, that experiences had convinced them that Jesus was not a dead prophet but a living presence who had disclosed himself to them in striking ways and whose spirit had taken possession of them. Upon this conviction the world mission of Christianity was founded, and upon it also was based the Christian hope for sharing Christ's triumph over death. Such religious arguments are valid, however, only for those who accept the basic assumption of the Christian position, but for such they are of great consequence.

WILL IT MAKE A DIFFERENCE?

When faced with the question, what difference will it make whether or not men believe in immortality, many people immediately jump to the conclusion that were it not for the deterrent exercised by men's belief in heaven and hell, people would quickly adopt the philosophy, "Eat, drink, and be merry for tomorrow we die," throw discretion to the winds and undertake a life of indulgence. Such, however, is not a thoughtful conclusion. In the first place, our ideas of right and wrong are very largely the product of human experience. Our moral codes do not represent the decrees of the Divine Being concerning the conditions of a blessed immortality, but are the product of long social experimentation. The things which society has concluded are wrong are those things which are seen to militate against the best interests of life here and now, and likewise those things deemed right are things which experience has shown contribute to the greater well-being of life in the world. Religion has underwritten these products of human experience with divine sanctions. The idea that men would quickly revert to evil in the event of the loss of belief in immortality is based upon the false assumption that in this present life evil is both more fascinating and rewarding than good. It is the very nature of evil to make it appear so, but the experience of men has again and again denied the truth of this proposition.

The question is not whether or not morals would lose their foundation, but how would the incentives and purposes of life be affected by denial of immortality. Men would not begin to wallow in the mire, or turn from decency to filth. But would they be moved to make those personal sacrifices that are the price of attaining the highest possibilities in the realm of character? It is one thing to concede the necessity of living decently, and another to justify the cultivation of the highest in honor and integrity when such attainment is possible only through great sacrifice of immediate benefits. If personal character is no more permanent than the body, will it justify the sacrifices required of those who would attain those higher realms which transcend accepted standards of society? Would true moral saintliness be worth its cost in self-discipline and self-denial?

Will it not make a difference what we do with our lives, if we consider present existence as all there is for us, or whether this life is but the initial stage of something far greater? If a man builds a house to serve only a few years and then be destroyed, he should seek to make it interesting and beautiful, but wood would suffice as building material. If, however, he is building for the ages, he will pay the price of stone, that his structure may combine beauty and endurance. Even so, if we are building characters for eternity there must be no insecure portions in the structures, and the cost involved in making all parts permanently secure in the beginning will be far less than that of reconstructing them later. The more costly attainments in character are justified only on the prospect of permanence.

CHAPTER XII

Why the Church?

FREQUENTLY religious leaders are asked the question, "Is it not possible to be a Christian outside of the church?" Usually the question hopes to establish the proposition that church membership is not essential to the Christian life. A more significant question would be, "Could religion as expressed in Christianity or Judaism survive without a church?" When the question is put this way most people will recognize that without the church religion of this type would soon perish. So necessary is it to a life of religion that if it were destroyed today it would spring up anew tomorrow, if not under the same name, at least to fulfill the same functions.

Before considering the necessary functions served by the church, it may be well to take account of varied conceptions of the church. The Roman Catholic view is clear and definite. The catechism defines the church as, "The congregation of all the faithful on earth, professing the true Faith, governed by their lawful Bishops and united under one visible Head." According to this view there is only one church and this a divinely established institution vested with the authority of Christ in the earth. Christ is its invisible head, but he conferred upon Peter his authority to serve as visible head of the church and the bishops of Rome are the lawful successors of Peter in this position and they have carried the title, the Holy Father, or Pope. As the Bishop of Rome is the successor to Peter, so the other bishops of the church are the successors of the other apostles. The priests are the authorized assistants of the bishops. These successors to the apostles are to serve as teachers, priests, and pastors, that is, they are to preach Christ's doctrine, administer the sacraments, and guide and rule the faithful. It is through the sacraments that the Grace of Christ is mediated to men. The sacraments are seven in number, Baptism, Confirmation, Holy Eucharist, Penance, Extreme Unction, Holy Orders, and Matrimony. As the sacraments can be administered only by priests, properly ordained in the apostolic succession, the conclusion is that apart from the church there can be no salvation. The church is the sole mediator of the merits wrought by Christ's sacrifice.

There is no accepted Protestant view of the church. The conceptions range from virtual agreement with the Catholic view that the church is a supernatural institution projected from heaven to that of a purely human fellowship. High-Church Episcopalians uphold the Catholic view of the church and differ from the Roman Catholic position only in their rejection of the Bishop of Rome as the visible head of the church on earth. This group recognizes three great branches of the church, namely the Anglican or Episcopalian, the Eastern Orthodox, and the Roman Catholic, which are said to agree in the essentials of faith and worship. At the other extreme, is the Society of Friends who do not use the term church but whose societies fulfill like functions. For these the church represents a purely human fellowship. One outstanding Protestant declares that the sanction for the church is found "not in supernatural dictation but in the psychological and social necessities of human life." As an intermediate position the Augsburg Confession, the doctrinal foundation of Lutheranism, may be cited which declares, "The church is the congregation of the saints in which the gospel is rightly taught and the sacraments rightly administered." The Westminster Confession recognizes a church universal which is invisible and comprises the whole number of the elect. The visible church "consists of all those throughout the world that profess the true religion and of their children." Ordinarily, according to this document, there is no possibility of salvation out of the church. In general, Protestantism regards all its separate divisions as churches and in practice thinks in terms of churches rather than "the church." This last is especially true in denominations which adhere to congregational polity in government in which each local organization is held to be a church.

In view of the concerted effort going forward in Christendom to bring to pass a union of Christian denominations into a united church, much attention is being given in contemporary thought to rethinking the doctrine of the church. This concentration upon the problem is having its effect as is revealed in an utterance of a former editor of a leading religious journal who is himself a product of a congregational tradition but who has come to visualize the church in other terms. Says Charles Clayton Morrison, "I hold that the Christian church is a unique emergent in history, that it is not a humanly devised institution, that it is not in the world by virtue of man's making it, or imagining it, or even feeling the need of it, but that it is here by the will and grace of God."[1]

Inasmuch as there is no accepted Protestant view of the church, we must be content pending further thought and consultation with noting the distinguishing marks of Protestantism which may be summarized in brief as, the rejection of the authority of the Roman hierarchy, the principle of salvation by faith, the priesthood of all believers which makes unnecessary a mediator between man and God, the acknowledgment of the Bible as the final authority in questions of Christian faith and practice, and the right of private judgment in interpreting the scriptures.

FUNCTIONS OF THE CHURCH

To return to the original question, "Why is a church essential to the life of the Christian religion?" it is possible to point out an all-inclusive function and a number of secondary ones that belong to this institution. The comprehensive responsibility of the church is to witness to its faith in the world. All other functions are subsidiary to this one and the test of justification for any particular activity in the church's program is, does the activity contribute to the effective witness of the church to its faith.

Perhaps the first of the subsidiary functions to be realized in the church was the creation of a religious fellowship. Whenever men have been the subjects of creative religious experience, their first impulse has always been to share this experience with others and to create a fellowship around the new religious ideal. In this way great religions have been born, such as Zoroastrianism, Buddhism, Confucianism, Moham-

---

[1] *The Christian Century,* Editorial, May 12, 1937.

medanism, Judaism and Christianity. This theme is repeated in the founding of the Christian sects or denominations. When one thinks of the Lutheran Church he recalls the experiences of Martin Luther. Back of the Presbyterian and Reformed churches is the experience of John Calvin; of the Quakers, George Fox; of the Methodists, John Wesley; of the Disciples, Alexander Campbell. The impulse to form associations on the basis of commonly accepted beliefs and ideals is irrepressible. In such fellowship individuals aware of their own insufficiency gain moral and religious support and as a united society they become potent factors in the life of the larger community. It is of the nature of religion to crave fellowship.

A second function which requires but little comment is that of religious education. The principal task here is the transmission of the religious heritage from generation to generation so that it may be fully understood and its essential experiences renewed in the lives of new adherents. The main task is in connection with the rising generation, but inasmuch as there is always room for further enlightenment, the program of religious education must include all ages and classes. A curriculum must include the contents of the sacred writings, the history of the institutions, the lives of the great representatives, the essential doctrines, the moral ideals and the application of these truths to the problems of life. Although other institutions are deeply interested in character development, no other institution is committed to the fulfillment of these tasks which are included under the religious education program of the church.

Religions which maintain their highest vitality must propagate themselves and add to the number of their adherents. A lack of growth is interpreted as indicative of decline. As the third function of the church we may designate the propagation of the faith through programs of evangelism or missionary activity of various kinds where the ultimate goal is to win converts to the particular religion. The methods may be various but the goal in view is the winning of new adherents to religion which the church represents.

A fourth function of the church may be called the pastoral. This represents the effort of the church to bring help to individuals in the solution of their personal problems. Some of its commonest forms are the ministry of comfort in the time of sorrow and of encouragement in the time of disappointment. Frequently it expresses itself in the help afforded the individual in making important moral decisions, or in the endeavor to bring light to bear upon the problem of the determination of one's vocation. More and more the churches are looked to for a helpful ministry in the realm of psychotherapy, helping people to overcome mental and social maladjustments and particularly to help straighten out tangled domestic relations. This service of personal guidance oftentimes referred to as "the cure of souls" seems to be gaining a new prominence in the present age of social confusion.

WORSHIP

One of the functions of the church which has been minimized at least in Protestant circles, but which seems to be coming into its own again, in the modern age, is that of worship. Worship is another of those vital terms like life and religion which eludes accurate definition. In general, however, it may be said that religious worship means consciously entering the presence of God for the purpose of manifesting reverence, adoration, and devotion, and to see life under divine perspective. Through the medium of prayer, worship may be a private act, but in this chapter on the church and its functions our concern is with corporate worship.

What are the motives which lead people to participation in corporate worship? It may be well to consider first of all those motives which are subject to criticism. These have already been discussed to some extent in connection with the question, why are people religious, in the initial chapter of this work, but it will be profitable, however, to mention specifically two or three of these urges in the present discussion.

QUESTIONABLE MOTIVES

One motive for engaging in worship which will scarcely bear the light of reason is that of rendering to God his due. This mode of thought pictures God as demanding worship for his own gratification and as offended if the reverence and honor which is due him is withheld. God stands on his dignity demanding the adulation due a king. Men should worship, therefore, in order to avoid God's wrath. Giving God his due in worship is like paying taxes for the support of the government. If one attempts to withhold the payment of taxes from the government, he can expect to be prosecuted and punished therefor. As one pays his taxes in order to avoid trouble, so he engages in worship in order to keep God appeased and avoid his wrath. The conception of God involved in this mode of reason scarcely accords with the teachings of Jesus concerning the nature of God's love for men.

The second questionable motive for engaging in worship is the seeking of heightened emotional experiences for their own sake. Some people make use of worship as the means of going on an emotional spree. The writer has attended services where, apparently, the whole desire of those in attendance was to have their feelings so stimulated that the normal rational controls of life would be inhibited and they would break over in unusual manifestation such as strange ecstatic utterances, designated as speaking with tongues, and various kinds of emotional seizures. These phenomena were interpreted as evidences that they had received "the power," that their lives were being stimulated by the divine afflatus, and that in this experience they had attained a union with the holy spirit. These experiences were cherished for their own sakes and bore no relationship to the ordinary activities or problems of daily life. There are others of more refined taste, who are repelled by these crude manifestations of the religious impulse, who are content to seek out aesthetic experiences for their own sake. They may seek to lose themselves in the rapture of great music or in the glow of stimulated emotion, but as in the previous case these experiences have no end beyond the delights of the moment. There is good reason for thinking that such experiences sought for their own sake without relation to the real problems of life are debilitating in their effect upon moral character and therefore not to be encouraged.

More serious still is the result when one deliberately engages in a worship experience as a means of escape from life's hard facts, disappointments, and discouragements. Sometimes religion is used as a means of running away from life's realities and finding compensation in the realm of sweet illusions. No worship is justified which encourages man to run away from life's difficult problems.

LEGITIMATE MOTIVES

Worship must be positive in its results in the characters of men and should contribute to their effectiveness in dealing with the realities of living. Worship should be an experience of reorientation of the lives of individuals about the central meaning and purpose of all existence. It should be the means by which man regains a true perspective, accomplishes the revaluation of values, and effects the organization of life about its central purpose. According to H. N. Wieman, "Worship is the time when a man deliberately undertakes to make the best possible adjustment to that which he believes in all sincerity to be the matter of greatest concern." In order to see all the lesser elements of life in their true perspective, man turns his attention in worship from those lesser things to a consideration of that which is of supreme importance. He seeks not to run away from reality but to discover that deeper reality from which all lesser concerns derive their significance in order that he may see all the elements of life in their proper proportion.

Life seems to require, if it is to be lived at its best, the establishment of a rhythm in which alternately one turns his attention away from the many lesser concerns of the daily round to that inclusive end which gathers in itself all of these particular matters and infuses them with meaning. Professor Hocking refers to this need as the Principle of Alternation.[2] Over-prolonged attention to daily tasks and the details that make up our existence causes them to lose their significance and tends to exhaust man's zest for living and achieving. Life goes stale under such conditions. To recover the lost enthusiasm man must cease straining and striving, turn his attention away from life's particulars and contemplate its wholeness and its central meaning in a mood of relaxation and receptivity. A new sense of the whole so gained will re-infuse the particulars with meaning. But as too long a period of striving is self-defeating by robbing man of his incentive to work, so too long a period of relaxation and receptivity will also prove disastrous. The mystic experience loses its sense of reality when the endeavor is made to continue it indefinitely. Life finds its best expression in a rhythm of alternation between work and worship.

The need for establishing this rhythm of life is particularly apparent in the experience of the modern student, inasmuch as his life tends to be pulled apart by a wide diversity of interests which frequently are poorly correlated to one another. He may begin his day with a class in French at eight, one in mathematics at nine, and another in geology

---

[2] *Meaning of God in Human Experience*, Chap. 28. Yale Univ. Press.

at ten. The relationship of these to one another is not always visible. Following a variety of classes and studies he feels the lure of a program of extra-curricular activities, success in which will win him recognition and good standing among his fellows. So he may endeavor to express himself in athletics, music, dramatics, journalism, politics, and fraternity and social interests, and become "a big man on the campus." Each of these interests will take their toll of time and energy, and the student finds he must hurry from one to another with little opportunity for reflection.

Such a harried life is bound to wear out enthusiasm quickly unless provision is made for regular recuperation. Such recovery requires more than physical rest and harmless diversion although these make important contributions to the banishing of ennui. But more important for keeping life well integrated and effectively directed is real worship in which life's greater meanings reassert themselves and its larger goals resume command. "Worship," says Professor Hocking, "is the self-conscious part of the natural recovery of value."

ADVANTAGES OF CORPORATE WORSHIP

In worship is there any advantage in the corporate type as compared with individual prayer and meditation? Most effective living probably requires both inasmuch as there are advantages in the corporate experience not to be found in private prayer. In the first place, the architecture in a well-appointed church will itself have a subduing effect on the spirit of one who enters and will help to evoke the feeling of personal humility, which is a prerequisite to transferring attention from self to the wholeness of reality. Art expressed in windows of stained glass, in wall decorations, chancel appointments, and in beautiful symbols makes its unique contribution to an atmosphere conducive to the worship experience. The music of the service is another important factor in inducing an inner spirit favorable to the contemplation of the highest realities. In addition to the contribution of the fine arts in creating an atmosphere highly favorable to the worship experience, there is the advantage of associations of time and place. When certain experiences become habitual in relation to specified times and places, it ceases to be difficult to induce them because they have become part of one's nature. Regular services of worship in a sanctuary dedicated to that purpose become a great help to those who would establish the habit.

A third advantage in corporate worship is that of contagion. That which may be difficult by one's self alone may become easy and natural when engaged in with others and all act together. Through the singing of hymns, the offering of common prayers and participation in the sacraments, a common spirit infuses the whole body of worshipers, which should provide the condition for real worship experience on the part of each individual. There is danger here, of course, of establishing a crowd psychology in which the individual loses his identity and becomes the easy prey of suggestion. To avoid this result no attempt should be made to hypnotize the worshiper, and this need not occur if the worship is conducted with dignity, on the basis of high thinking, and in ways that permit and encourage individual reflection. When this is done the contagion of the group is a real asset rather than a liability.

A final advantage in group worship is that of leadership. Leading in worship is a fine art for which many ministers have been poorly trained. By reason of this lack ministers frequently are themselves guilty of depriving their congregations of the richness inherent in vital worship. But when a minister has a true sense of his responsibility and some ability in executing it, he can direct the thoughts and feelings of the congregation in ways that will bring them into the very presence of God and enable them to experience a renewal of life on a spiritual plane.

SOME WORSHIP EXPERIENCES

We have already spoken of worship as a means of reorienting life to its central meaning and purpose, and it remains to take note of some specific ways in which lives have been affected by this experience. One common experience among worshipers is an exaltation of spirit which lifts one out of life's doldrums and above the depressing consciousness of immediate sordid facts to a vantage point of vision in which he contemplates the higher beauties of life and gains a restored sense of the supremacy of spiritual forces. This is not escape from reality, but is a means of gaining a new appreciation of the higher realities through which one sees life's distressing facts from a new perspective and is able to assume a saner attitude toward them. This experience may come as a contribution of the music, perhaps when familiar tunes rich in associations are played in the pure tones of the chimes to soft organ accompaniment and awaken anew the sense of reality in the spiritual. Or it may be that while listening to a glorious anthem one is lifted into a higher plane of existence than his customary dwelling and receives a new insight into the possibilities of life. In the midst of such experiences one feels as did Peter, James and John on the Mount of Transfiguration when Peter exclaimed, "Master, it is good for us to be here," and he goes back to the work-a-day world refreshed in spirit.

A second familiar experience in worship is to be overcome with a consciousnness of sin and of those moral failures which stand in the way of a person realizing his best self. This realization may come in connection with the prayer of confession, or in quiet moments of meditation when a person reviews his own actions in retrospect, or as an effect of the sermon. Under such circumstances people have become keenly aware of situations in which they manifested an ugly disposition to their shame, or of others in which they were carried away by selfish desires. In such moments they have become conscious of incidents when they were particularly inconsiderate of the feelings of others and hurt them unnecessarily. The consciousness of such failures and the resulting determination not to give way to these same impulses in similar situations is undoubtedly an important factor in the refining of personal character. The saints are those who through the repetition of such experiences have kept their consciences highly sensitized.

Another effect of the worship experience is to make men aware of their common humanity by breaking down the artificial barriers that separate them from each other. The writer has witnessed a dignified university president kneel before an altar in company with a lowly man of labor to receive the elements of the communion. No one who was a party of that scene could go forth and immediately set himself above his fellows as being better than they. An awareness of the fact that we are creatures of God with common needs as we stand before him draws us together into a realization of our fundamental brotherhood. Douglas Steere in his *Prayer and Worship* tells of happenings that have come under his own observation in the silence of Quaker meetings. Among other things he states: "For those who actively participate in this form of corporate inward prayer, there is often a melting down, a tendering, in which each feels very closely knit to the common Father and to his fellows. I have seen this silent worship level a group in which there was an ugly barrier separating two of its members, and I have seen it bring them to ask forgiveness."[3] In worship many a person has gained a new appreciation of his fellows.

A fourth experience frequently had in the course of worship is a new stimulation to a high consecration of life. How often in the midst of worship some great ideal lays its claim upon us, or a great cause summons us to enlist under its banners and join the ranks of its champions. As has already been indicated the experience of being claimed by some high truth, beauty or goodness to which one dedicates himself willingly is religious experience par excellence. More frequently than not it is in the midst of effective corporate worship that such consecrations occur in response to a clear vision of what life may mean if given to the making real of some new possibility.

The subject of worship has been treated at some length because it is one of the functions of the church which young people too little appreciate and too often neglect. There is yet another function of the church to be considered, its obligation to witness to its faith in connection with the social order. As this subject presents a problem on which there are decided differences of opinion among the churches, it too must be accorded a fuller discussion which is reserved for the next chapter.

[3] P. 49 f.

CHAPTER XIII

Religion and Social Change

HOW shall the church witness to its faith in relation to the social order? No question is causing greater disturbance within church constituencies, unless it be the problem of the church's many divisions. The question is does the church have a responsibility in connection with the character of social, political and economic institutions and practices; and if it does, what are the legitimate and what are improper methods of discharging that responsibility? On these matters there is no unanimity of conviction.

FUNDAMENTALIST POSITION

The prevalent attitudes found in the church with respect to the social question seem to divide into three approaches to the problem. The first group maintains that the church has no business concerning itself with the structure of the social order for that is entirely beyond its province. The world as such is an evil order which God has renounced. Evil forces are in control and through their activities the world is bound to grow worse rather than better and it would be as foolish for the church to try to transform the social order as to try to brush back the tide with a broom. When the situation gets bad enough God will intervene to judge the world, the present era will come to an end in a terrible manifestation of God's wrath, and Christ will return to establish his Kingdom in place of the earthly kingdoms now ruling. A certain satisfaction is taken by "the saved" in the growing evil of the world, for the more evil the world grows the sooner will occur the judgment and the return of Christ to rule.

For those who accept the view that the church has no responsibility for the structure of the social order, its function is not to save the world for Christ but to save men out of a world that is hopelessly corrupt. Their gospel is one of individual deliverance and their goal to save men from the inevitable destruction impending for all who do not accept the salvation which Christ has provided for those who put their faith in him. Their task is to pluck brands from the burning. To be sure they may protest against certain acknowledged evils, such as the liquor traffic, organized vice, or Sunday evening movies when these entice young people away from the church and from following paths of personal rectitude, but there is no effort made to effect changes in the underlying social or economic structure. Such is the attitude of those Christians who call themselves Fundamentalists.

A CONSERVATIVE VIEW

A position that is properly labeled conservative does not abandon the world to the devil and his forces as beyond all hope of improvement. The advocates of this view, however, join the fundamentalists in asserting that the message of the church is for individuals and its duty is to mold the character of individuals. Its effect on social institutions should be wholly indirect and should operate through the influence and activities of individuals who have been redeemed and have accepted Christlike ideals through the ministry of the church. Only good men can make a good society and it is the business of the church to make men good and then the social order will take care of itself. When the church endeavors by direct action to affect the nature of the social and economic structure it acts entirely outside its proper sphere and by its meddling and tampering does more harm than good in the society it would transform. What is more serious it corrupts its own nature, loses its holiness and sanctity, becomes contaminated with worldliness, and loses its ability to function as a medium of divine grace to spiritually hungry men.

This point of view has received vigorous expression through the words of J. Howard Pew, a Presbyterian layman and former president of the Sun Oil Company. He served as chairman of the National Lay Committee, a group of 190 prominent laymen, who were appointed in 1950 to serve as a sponsoring group for the newly organized National Council of Churches. The committee was not an integral part of the structure of the National Council, nor was it designed to be permanent, but was appointed to help launch the new organization and enlist adequate support for it. When the committee was dissolved in 1955, Mr. Pew addressed a letter to the members in which he voiced the following judgments:

Throughout our Committee's term of life, it repeatedly brought to the Council's attention the seriousness of the problems involved in its issuance of controversial statements and studies in the fields of sociology, economics and politics; and the danger inherent in speaking to official Washington and the United Nations General Assembly in behalf of Protestantism on matters outside their field and for which they possessed no mandate.

. . .

The members of the Lay Committee were often misunderstood in their urgency to keep the churches out of politics and their insistence on the primacy of evangelism. Our premise was that instead of appealing to the government, the church should devote its energies to the work of promoting the attributes of Christianity—truth, honesty, fairness, generosity, justice and charity in the hearts and minds of men. We attempted to emphasize that Christ stressed not the expanded state but the dignity and responsibility of the individual.[1]

It was the contention of Mr. Pew that economic and political controversies have "no moral and ethical content," and, therefore, are not proper concerns of the churches and the National Council.

A similar point of view was championed some years ago by another prominent industrialist and former Governor of Missouri, the late Arthur M. Hyde:

If the Sermon on the Mount means what it says, Christianity is a matter of the individual. Its essence is the proper relationship of man to God, its application a proper relationship of man to man. But always it is an individual relationship. . . . Christianity, we are taught to believe, cares for us as individuals; its supreme achievement is the building of character; it reacts upon the social structure, influences and molds the social system in which it exists, through the lives and works of such characters.

. . .

It is men who do wrong not systems.[2]

[1] *U. S. News and World Report,* Feb. 3, 1956, p. 47.
[2] *The Forum,* Vol. XCIV, Nov. 1935, p. 268; Vol. XCV, Jan. 1936, p. vi.

Although not stated as specifically as it might be by the laymen, one of the great fears of the conservatives in this controversy is that by reason of its implication in the affairs of the world the church will lose its essential character as a church and become a secularized institution unable to minister to spiritual need. The danger is real and no doubt one of the most serious indictments that can be brought against the church of our day is that it has been too largely infected with secularism. The reasons for this are several and not simply its activities in the field of social action.

SECULARISM

What is meant by charging the church with secularism? It must be recognized that every great institution will reflect certain characteristics of the culture in which it takes its rise. Even a church cannot exist in cultural isolation from its environment. When it becomes a thing apart it loses its power to influence the members of the cultural group. A certain amount of adaptation on the part of the church to the world is inevitable. Religion can no more separate itself from general culture than can music, art or literature. To do so would be to forfeit reality. But religion ought also to be a powerful factor in determining the character of any culture, either indirectly through the influence of individuals whom it reaches, or more directly through concerted and corporate action. The church becomes guilty of secularism when it is more concerned to adapt itself to the ways of the world in order to find favor with the world than it is to be a decisive factor in molding the character of that world in line with the gospel. There is a very real sense in which the church must be in the world, but not of it. As Reinhold Niebuhr has expressed it, "The particular peril of the established church is to be held in too intimate an embrace by the established order." In totalitarian countries the churches have virtually lost their independence and must be subservient to the demands of the state. In democratic countries the charge is made that the church has become a bulwark of an evil status quo and has largely lost independence of spirit without being conscious of its bondage. For this condition of subservience to the world the conservatives blame the advocates of the social gospel in swerving the church from its proper purposes, whereas the latter lay the blame largely at the door of the conservatives who by their social blindness have unwittingly divorced the church from reality. Wherever the fault may lie it is true that the church has lost much of its power as a redemptive force and creative element and has succumbed too much to the overpowering influences of the contemporary world and needs to recover its independence. It must reorient itself about its own essential faith and be a more effective witness to that faith.

AN AGGRESSIVE POLICY

A third prevailing attitude within the church with respect to its responsibility for the social order may be termed the aggressive. Advocates of this position join the issue with the conservatives, and it will be well to recount the answers they give to the latters' charges. Words once spoken by the late Bishop Francis J. McConnell express the essence of the matter:

It is the duty of the church to take account of all the forces which help or hinder the building of individual character. It appears at once that the social forces take on profound significance for shaping individual lives— and because of such power are inevitably objects of concern to the church. This is the more important because the church is herself a social institution with power to help make that social climate whose meaning for individual development we are more and more coming to realize. The real aim of present-day Christian social effort is to create social conditions which will give individuals a better chance at any liberty worth having.[3]

The basic criticism which the aggressives make of the conservatives is that they fail to comprehend the true nature of the relationship between the individual and society. It is impossible to isolate individuals from society except physically. To attempt it would be to destroy the individual, for no person can develop himself in a social vacuum. Only through a process of interaction with other beings with like nature and capacities does a personality develop. Society is the name given to that complex pattern of interaction between persons. As there is no such thing as an isolated individual, culturally speaking, so there is no such thing as an abstract society. The two terms refer to two essential aspects of an ongoing process which cannot be separated from each other. What affects soccety inevitably affects the individuals who compose

[3] *Ibid.*, p. 270.

that society, and whatever affects individuals will have consequences for the total society. To set up an individual gospel over against a social gospel represents a false dichotomy. There is—or should be—but one gospel with implications for men as individuals and in social relations.

In the very situations which the conservatives declare to be without moral content, the defenders of an aggressive attitude find tremendous ethical values at stake because of the nature of their impact on individual persons. Some years ago a group of prominent Methodist laymen sought to restrict the tendency toward a program of social action which was growing up in their communion. Among their declarations was the following:

> Economic and social systems operate upon mankind in the mass. They are the result of social evolution throughout the centuries. In themselves they are mechanistic in character, impersonal in operation, and not primarily interested in men and women, nor in their hopes, aspirations, or characters.

"What more serious indictment of existing systems from the standpoint of a Christian standard could you ask!" the antagonists would reply. They would affirm that any system which is completely indifferent and oblivious to "the hopes, aspirations, or characters" of people represents the antithesis of Judaic-Christian values and must be modified until it subserves them.

Much more pungent than the remarks of Bishop McConnell already quoted in criticism of the conservative position were declarations made about the same time by Charles Clayton Morrison, then the editor of *The Christian Century*. In a sermon before a pastors' institute he declared that the teachings of Jesus have been studied for two generations with an intense devotion with the result that no generation has known the Sermon on the Mount as our generation knows it. At the same time we have been inquiring into the nature of our economic and political society. The result of this twofold study has been "solemnizing." He declared:

> We have discovered, first, that the Christian church does not seriously believe in practicing the ethics of Jesus and, second, that the ethics of Jesus cannot be practiced in the kind of world in which we live. . . . Certainly the naïve assumption that we can sit at the feet of Jesus on the Galilean hillside, listen to his teaching about the law of love, and go straightway to

practice that law in our daily life—that naïve assumption is now seen to be an illusion. Christian people do not practice the ethics of Jesus and they are awaking to the fact that they cannot do so. The kind of world in which we live requires us to do things which contradict Christ's teachings.

As a further result of study into the nature of contemporary society it becomes evident that "secular society as now organized damns men's souls faster than evangelical Christianity can save them." As a solution of the dilemma in which this situation puts those who would be loyal to Christ he makes the following suggestion:

If the law of love is not practicable as things now are, we are beginning to see that it is the imperative task of Christianity to change conditions so that the law of love will be practicable. . . . Under the mandate of Jesus' law of love we must make a new world in which his law of love can be practiced. The kingdoms of this world—the kingdoms of economics, of the political state, of industry and merchandising, of art and education—all the kingdoms of our secular culture—these must be made the Kingdom of our Lord and of his Christ. But to set about the making of such a world is itself to practice the teaching of Jesus. When once we commit ourselves to the task of building an earthly social order in which the will of God may be done as it is done in heaven, we have no ground left for asserting that Christ's law is impracticable, for by our effort to construct such a world we are actually engaged in practicing the law of love.[4]

In the acceptance of this challenge Christians will find a powerful motivation for the development of the inner, or spiritual life, for the achievement of such a goal will be possible only as men avail themselves of great spiritual resources. To follow such a program is not an invitation to the church to abandon its spiritual ministry but mightily to deepen that ministry.

Despite the criticisms of Mr. Pew and other members of his Lay Committee the National Council of Churches through its various divisions has from time to time published statements expressing judgments on current issues in which Christian values seemed to be at stake. As the rationale which underlies such pronouncements one may cite a statement adopted by the General Board of the National Council in September 1954 entitled "Christian Principles and Assumptions for

[4] "The Crisis in Christianity." *The Christian Century,* Sept. 26, 1934.

Economic Life." This statement was the product of extensive consultation on the part of more than one hundred Christian leaders including economists, labor leaders and businessmen, as well as theologians. The introduction begins with these paragraphs:

Christian churches have as a prime objective their ministry to individuals, and therefore have also a basic relationship and responsibility to the societies which they seek to serve. Their role in that society has two aspects.

One of their responsibilities is the conservation and promotion in that society of such values as justice and freedom.

The other responsibility is prophetic, in the scriptural sense of trying to view all human relations and institutions in the light of the teachings of the gospel. It involves leadership in the continuous struggle so to improve what is that it moves toward what ought to be, according to that standard. This means pointing out and trying to correct imperfections and abuses.

After acknowledging the difficulty involved in exercising the prophetic role, the statement continues:

Yet the churches dare not abandon the prophetic role. To do so would be to yield leadership for peace and freedom and justice and to disregard the churches' mandatory responsibility under the gospel. When we cease to strive and speak for a society based upon these values, we give the impression that we have ceased to care about them.

QUESTIONS OF STRATEGY

The aggressive group have chosen to follow a dangerous course, but in its creative periods religion has always involved itself in great dangers. To avoid disaster the church must be wise in its choice of methods and carefully determine its strategy. In considering what the church may justifiably do to render the social order more Christian in its operation, it may be well to note certain things which it may not do if it is not to jeopardize its existence as a church competent to minister to men's spiritual needs. The church should never identify itself with a political party or general political program. There is room for honest difference of belief about such matters among sincere followers of Christ, and in the church all sincere Christians should feel equally at home. The same is true with respect to economic systems. The flawless economic system has not yet been created. It should be remembered also that it is easier to discern the faults of a system already in operation than of one which exists mostly in theory and has not been put to the test of practice. The church must respect conscientious differences of opinion in these regards. The church's concern is not with systems as such, but with upholding certain moral principles whatever the system, such as justice, love, freedom, brotherhood, the responsibility of the strong for the weak and the primacy of personal values.

It follows from what has been said that the church should not seek to control or run the government. A free church within a free state has proven itself to be a good principle even though it is not always simple to apply. The church may properly seek to influence governmental action when moral issues plainly are at stake, but when it seeks to make civil government a function of the church the result is always disastrous for church and state alike. If it is not the business of the church to run the government, neither should it go into business and seek to control industry. It has the right to speak when industry flaunts its ideals, but it is not competent to direct industry and will bring contempt upon itself if it attempts it.

THE PROPHETIC FUNCTION

As already suggested among the things which the church may properly do in exerting a redemptive influence on the social order is to exercise a prophetic function. For this there is good and ancient precedent carrying back to the early periods of the Bible. A prophet is the spokesman of God who voices the judgment of God on contemporary practices of the people. Where prevailing practices in any realm of human behavior deny the standards which God has ordained it is the business of the prophet to bring the pertinent facts into clear light and to point out to society the dire consequences that are bound to follow if people persist in their evil ways. It is the business of the prophet to arouse the social conscience with respect to the evils of the day and to goad men into action in the effort to eradicate those evils before they involve society in unmitigated disasters. Where policies of government or industry, or where accepted social customs contradict the values and standards which the church is dedicated to uphold, the church to be true to itself must speak out courageously its disapproval and through the influence of its membership seek to change the practices into conformity to its own ideals.

When the church fails to express a judgment upon immoral goals or practices in government by saying that political concerns are none of its business, it stands in grave danger of being reduced to a condition of subserviency to a pagan state, and of being so controlled by that state that it will find it impossible to fulfill its essential functions. It will be limited to such innocuous activities as will not obstruct the state in any way in carrying forward its evil purposes. In very large measure such was the situation of the church in Germany under the Hitler regime, and of the church in Russia today.

Rabbi Abba Hillel Silver speaks so powerfully of the prophetic function of religion and its justification that his words deserve to be quoted at some length:

The religious man will be driven by the dynamics of his faith to a morality of battle and struggle. The axioms of faith lead to tremendous ethical mandates. Every human life must be regarded as a reflex of divinity. Every act of wrong and injustice, therefore, mars and defaces the image of God in man. Oppression and exploitation are more than violations of social laws. They are sacrilege and blasphemy. They thwart life—God's life in man. They distort and mutilate that which is the end and goal of all being—the free unfoldment of personality. The religious man will not rest content with personal salvation. He will strive to bring about a social order which will insure to all men freedom for self-realization. He will weigh all social institutions in the balance of spiritual utility. If found wanting, he will set about to reconstruct them, or, if need be, to destroy them. His morality will be militant, and, when necessary, revolutionary.

Hence it is that the profoundly religious men of all times were the mightiest spokesmen of social justice and its uncompromising champions. It was from the lips of men touched with the burning coal of divine faith, from the lips of the prophet, the seer, the man of God, that the first great cry for justice leaped out into the world. They who sought God most zealously spoke of human rights most fearlessly. It was in the name of God, the compassionate and merciful Friend, that they pleaded the cause of the orphan and the widow, the beaten and the broken of life.[5]

EDUCATIONAL ACTIVITIES

Closely related to the prophetic function of arousing the social conscience and moving men into action against corporate evils is the carry-

[5] *Religion in a Changing World*, pp. 55 f. Richard R. Smith, Inc., 1930.

ing on of social education that men may understand the nature of the forces that operate to determine the conditions of life. There are many things which churches may do in this area in addition to utterances by the minister from the pulpit. On controversial issues it may carry on a significant educational program more effectively apart from the pulpit and the services of worship. Discussion groups, study clubs, lectures, exhibits, and forums where each side of the case receives a fair presentation followed by general discussion, are all legitimate ways of educating the church community without bringing undue pressure to bear on anyone and without violation of conscience. Dramatic presentations and debates are yet other means. A very effective technique is that of educational and reconciliation trips where groups under careful guidance are taken actually to see conditions that are socially significant both as examples of situations calling for understanding and correction, and as illustrations of how certain problems may be solved. In many such ways the church may minister legitimately to the social education of its people and make them more effective as Christian citizens.

In addition to the foregoing activities which may be carried on by local churches other possibilities are open to churches acting together through local, regional or national councils. Local councils may encourage and assist one or more of the local clergy to keep well informed as to what is going on in the industrial field in the relations of management and labor, and to be used as resource persons by all the churches. In some instances it should be possible to provide a specialist for the area who would give full time to educating the churches on the one hand, and on the other to interpreting the bearing of religion upon problems of labor and management to their respective representatives. Through co-operative action the churches may also sponsor conferences, institutes and schools in which representatives of these concerns would meet with competent religious leaders to discover how to apply the principles of religion to their particular problems.

Beginning with a historic conference in Pittsburgh in 1947 the Department of the Church and Economic Life of the National Council of Churches has promoted on a national scope a series of significant conferences on problems related to economic life. Included in the membership of such conferences were church leaders, industrialists, merchants, bankers, labor leaders, agriculturalists, social scientists and educators. Subjects considered have included the general principles which should guide the activities of the churches in this area, and more specific problems, such as agricultural policy, labor-management relations, co-operatives and mutual business enterprises, and Christian vocation. The findings of these consultations have provided a significant series of monographs for study and further discussion by the churches, and have contributed to an enlightened public opinion with respect to these matters. What has been done in the field of economic life can also be done, and in a measure is being done, in other fields of social concern.

RESOLUTIONS AND PRONOUNCEMENTS

A policy involving somewhat greater dangers than those already mentioned, but legitimate if safeguarded against abuse, is that of making public pronouncements, the passing of resolutions, and the giving of endorsements to constructive measures of legislation. It is important in all such cases that clear moral issues be involved and that the public statements concern themselves only with the moral issues. The church must never allow itself to become the servant of a political faction in its effort to build political power or prestige. With parties it must have no concern, but where moral issues are at stake, it may speak.

In recent years many church bodies have adopted a set of social ideals. They are not set up as criteria by which to judge the standing of particular local parishes, or as qualifications for membership in the church, but they represent goals endorsed by the legislative representatives of the churches and become guides to the churches' endeavors along these lines. The best-known statement of this kind bears the title, "The Social Ideals of the Churches," and was adopted by the Federal Council of the Churches of Christ in America in 1932. It has exerted a large influence over the actions of various denominations in determining their own social goals, and may be regarded as a landmark in registering a new attitude on the part of the churches with respect to their responsibilities in seeking to influence the nature and forms of society. Although the document has had no official status since the Federal Council was succeeded by the National Council of Churches in 1950, as an example of the kind of goals which churches seek to realize it is worthy of quotation in full:

THE SOCIAL IDEALS OF THE CHURCHES

The Churches Should Stand For:

1. Practical application of the Christian principle of social well-being to the acquisition and use of wealth, subordination of speculation and the profit motive to the creative and co-operative spirit.

2. Social planning and control of the credit and monetary systems and the economic processes for the common good.

3. The right of all to the opportunity for self-maintenance; a wider and fairer distribution of wealth; a living wage, as a minimum, and above this a just share for the worker in the product of industry and agriculture.

4. Safeguarding of all workers, urban and rural, against harmful conditions of labor and occupational injury and disease.

5. Social insurance against sickness, accident, want in old age and unemployment.

6. Reduction of hours of labor as the general productivity of industry increases; release from employment at least one day in seven, with a shorter working week in prospect.

7. Such special regulation of the conditions of work of women as shall safeguard their welfare and that of the family and the community.

8. The right of employees and employers alike to organize for collective bargaining and social action; protection of both in the exercise of this right; the obligation of both to work for the public good; encouragement of co-operatives and other organizations among farmers and other groups.

9. Abolition of child labor; adequate provision for the protection, education, spiritual nurture and wholesome recreation of every child.

10. Protection of the family by the single standard of purity; educational preparation for marriage, home-making and parenthood.

11. Economic justice for the farmer in legislation, financing, transportation and the price of farm products as compared with the cost of machinery and other commodities which he must buy.

12. Extension of the primary cultural opportunities and social services now enjoyed by urban populations to the farm family.

13. Protection of the individual and society from the social, economic and moral waste of any traffic in intoxicants and habit-forming drugs.

14. Application of the Christian principle of redemption to the treatment of offenders; reform of penal and correctional methods of institutions, and of criminal court procedure.

15. Justice, opportunity and equal rights for all; mutual goodwill and co-operation among racial, economic and religious groups.

16. Repudiation of war, drastic reduction of armaments, participation in

international agencies for the peaceable settlement of all controversies; the building of a co-operative world order.

17. Recognition and maintenance of the rights and responsibilities of free speech, free assembly, and a free press; the encouragement of free communication of mind with mind as essential to the discovery of truth.

Several references have been made to the National Council of Churches of Christ in the United States of America, which in 1950 succeeded the previous Federal Council and twelve other interdenominational agencies which prior to that time had operated independently. The Council is constituted by thirty-three member communions which have a total membershsip of 37,870,000. Its functions were greatly enlarged over those performed by the Federal Council; and it seeks to discharge these through four divisions and a number of service units, the divisions being Christian Education, Christian Life and Work, Home Missions and Foreign Missions. The Division of Life and Work sponsors a number of departments and commissions and among them there is one on International Affairs, one on Racial and Cultural Relations, and another, whose work has already been described in brief, the Church and Economic Life. Through these departments the Council seeks to guide the thought of the churches with respect to the spiritual and moral aspects involved in social, political and economic issues. Results of commission studies have been publicized and pronouncements have been made on a wide range of issues by these departments and by the General Board of the Council. These statements have been used not only as a means of informing the churches, but also in endeavors to influence legislative action and administrative policies relating to racial, industrial and international affairs.

As an example of the growing concern of the churches to have a voice in determining national policies which have a direct bearing on human welfare there may be cited the hearings before the Committee on Foreign Affairs of the House of Representatives, held on May 28, 29, and June 5, 1957, on The Mutual Security Act of 1957. The particular issue under discussion was United States foreign aid and technical assistance to undeveloped areas of the world. Among the persons who appeared before the committee were two representatives of the National Council of Churches, and sixteen representatives of other national religious bodies, Jewish, Catholic and Protestant.

The World Council of Churches, organized in Amsterdam in 1947, includes one hundred sixty-three member bodies, Protestant and Eastern Orthodox. This organization also seeks to make an impact on the solution of many problems confronting a divided world. It also sponsors various commissions, and one of the most important of these is the Commission of the Churches on International Affairs, frequently designated by the initials CCIA. The stated purpose of this commission is "to set up an efficient channel for bringing the impact of Christian ideals and standards into the realm of international relations." This and other interests received major attention at the Second Assembly of the World Council of Churches held in Evanston, Illinois, in August 1954. For the discussion of its essential concerns the Assembly was divided into seven sections and three of them were definitely in the area under consideration in this chapter, The Responsible Society in the World Perspective, International Affairs, and Integroup Relations. Each section drew up a report of its deliberations and recommendations for submission to the churches "for study and appropriate action." In addition to these documents the entire assembly adopted a set of resolutions dealing very briefly with the problem of Religious Freedom, and more extensively with International Affairs and Intergroup Relations. Simply to indicate the character of these resolutions a brief paragraph is quoted from those dealing with ethnic relations:

> In the matter of the church's task amid racial and ethnic tensions the Second Assembly of the World Council of Churches declares its conviction that segregation in all its forms is contrary to the gospel, and is incompatible with the Christian doctrine of man and with the nature of the church of Christ. The assembly urges the churches within its membership to renounce all forms of segregation or discrimination based on race, color or ethnic origin, and to work for their abolition within their own life and within society.[6]

While speaking of important declarations that have been made by various national and international church organizations, mention should also be made of a series of significant papal encyclicals issued by the Roman Catholic Church through the years. Perhaps the most notable of these was issued by Pope Leo XIII in 1891, entitled *Rerum Novarum,*

[6] Quoted from *The Christian Century,* Sept. 22, 1954, pp. 1157 f.

and to many it has become known as a "working man's charter." Through such statements, and through the activities of the National Catholic Welfare Conference in this country, this great church also seeks to make its influence felt in connection with problems affecting human welfare.

AFFILIATED ORGANIZATIONS AND SPECIALIZED AGENCIES

Affiliated with the churches are a number of organizations not identical with them, which may or may not be officially endorsed by them, which have as their goals the securing of certain changes in social structure and practices designed to bring them into closer accord with Christian ideals. Often these associations are made up of prophetic souls who are particularly sensitive to certain evils and who act from the best of spiritual motives in their aggressive attack upon those evils. They may desire to go farther or be more radical in their procedures than the church as a whole would approve. When such high-minded people acting from commendable motives organize to make themselves effective in combating a recognized evil, it is right and proper that they should receive the encouragement and perhaps official recognition from the churches. A number of temperance societies have been organizations of this type. The Legion of Decency, launched under Roman Catholic auspices but supported by many Protestants, has been an effective agency in improving the moral qualities of the motion pictures offered to the public. The Church Peace Union seeks to work through various religious groups for a greater measure of world order. The Fellowship of Reconciliation is an organization of religious pacifists who seek to witness to the effectiveness of nonviolent methods of resisting evil as an alternative to war. The National Religion and Labor Foundation is dedicated to building a closer relationship and mutual understanding between organized labor and organized religion of all faiths. Many voluntary social agencies could also be named which look mainly to church people for their membership and support and whose work deserves the good will of the churches.

Many denominations recognize or authorize social agencies within their own structure. The Church League for Industrial Democracy, while not officially a part of the Episcopal Church, functions in close relation to it, and its meetings are held coincident to those of the General Assembly. The Methodists maintain a Board of Social and Economic Relations, and the Congregational-Christian Church a Council for Social Action. Most of the major denominations sponsor similar agencies. The United Presbyterian Church in the U.S.A. sponsors an Institute of Industrial Relations which has gained wide recognition. The Roman Catholic Church in the United States sponsors the National Welfare Conference, which in turn maintains a Social Action Department, and the Union of American Hebrew Congregations likewise maintains a Commission on Social Action.

Through these affiliated organizations and specialized agencies much effective work is being done in behalf of Christian ideals in social living. No member of a church is required to belong to any one of these organizations, or to endorse the actions of the denominational agency in order to maintain good standing in the fellowship of the church. The church through its message furnishes the motivation and dynamic, but the actual work is done by organizations better designed for effective action than are local congregations. By encouraging such organizations the churches may generate a mighty force for righteousness without forfeiting essential churchly qualities.

THE INITIAL TASK

Despite the continued opposition of many fundamentalists and conservatives the trend of the times certainly is in the direction of the churches assuming a larger responsibility for helping to shape the forms and practices of social life into greater accord with the moral ideals and standards of religion. Before the churches can be most effective in social crusading, however, they must put their own house in order, for at too many points their practices fall short of their acknowledged ideals. Most of the denominations, even in the South, have adopted resolutions upholding in principle at least the decision of the United States Supreme Court with respect to ending segregation in the public schools, but the church in its practice remains one of the most completely segregated institutions in the land. The church, however, is capable of self-criticism, and in the statement previously cited by the General Board of the National Council of Churches on Christian Principles and Assumptions for Economic Life the following indictment is included:

The churches themselves own property, invest funds and employ labor. Often their policies have been no better than those which the church condemns in the secular world. Its divisions often reflect and seem to give a religious sanction to those divisions which are characteristic of society at large. In all these matters judgment should "begin at the house of God."

Until the church realizes within its own fellowship in fuller measure than exists today the ideals it desires to enthrone in society, it will not be a very effective agent in influencing the world. The church must strive first of all to become a true Christian community which will transcend national, racial and class boundaries and exhibit within its own life the kind of brotherhood and justice that it desires to prevail throughout society. When it achieves this it will be in position to move the world.

CHAPTER XIV

The Future of Religion

SPECULATION with respect to the future is always uncertain business as no one can take into account all the factors that are shaping the things to come in any field. Wherever life and energy surge in people, however, there is little disposition to rest content with living in the present. It is the lure of future possibilities that urges us on from effort to effort. But if we live for the future, we must take account of the future.

Although no one of sane mind would maintain that he can foresee the future in all its details, it is possible to know something of the future because many elements of it are already present. Not only will much of the present carry on into the future, but some of the new forces that will mark the new age are already present in embryonic stages, or as trends which are beginning to gather force and give promise of far-reaching development before exhausting themselves. With some of those trends which seem to be shaping the future this chapter is concerned. Most of them have been implied in the preceding chapters of the book, but now it is our task to gather them together and see what they indicate for the age ahead.

The old established religions of the world are today under fire and are being forced to warfare against new ideologies and pseudo-religions which are effectively commanding the devotion of many millions of people over the world. It is hardly likely that either side will win a quick and decisive victory in this struggle. In this discussion attention will be directed to this challenge as it confronts Christianity. That this struggle will be the most powerful factor affecting the nature of Christian thought and practice for the next generation can hardly be doubted.

To be sure the decisive victory of the United Nations in the world war gave fascism in its various forms a very great setback. Hitler, Mussolini and the Japanese war lords were liquidated and their powers taken over by the conquerors, but the ideologies which they championed and the methods by which they supported them are by no means dead, however, and under other names are a constant threat to the established order even in democratic America. The resurgence of the Ku Klux Klan and the founding of other like associations for the purpose of fomenting hate and terror are evidence enough that the spirit of fascism has taken root among us. Communism in turn has gained greatly in both power and influence over the world as a result of the Russian victory in the war.

THE NEW TOTALITARIANISMS AS RELIGIONS

Whatever the particular type political totalitarianisms tend either to renounce religion or to render it completely subservient to the purposes of the state or party. They become themselves substitutes for religion and may properly be called pseudo religions, inasmuch as they evoke from their followers a devotion remarkably similar to religious devotion. Their founders and leaders are accorded honors due to saviours. Communists worship at the bier of Lenin and thousands of people daily press to gaze upon the preserved features of their deliverer in a spirit of worshipful reverence.

During the Stalin regime in Russia his picture appeared everywhere and he was accorded what amounted to divine honors. At the forefront of Italian fascism stood Mussolini, more powerful than the Italian Emperor, then the titular head of the state, and the recipient of more deference from the Italian people than the Bishop of Rome, the acknowledged head of their church. Under National Socialism in Germany, although officially a Christian state, "Heil Hitler" was shouted on every possible occasion and the honors accorded him far outstripped those given to Jesus Christ.

These new ideologies have their philosophies of history and progress which are cosmic in their setting and represent the emergence and play of forces that are more-than-human in their origin of which the present leaders are only the human agents. As a confession of faith the Communists have the *Communist Manifesto* published in 1848 by Karl

Marx and Friedrich Engels. The German Nazis had as their great inspiration and guide Hitler's *Mein Kampf* in which the history of the movement, the objectives and steps in the program were all set forth. Such writings are as sacred to the devotees of these movements as is the Bible to Christians and may be properly regarded as their scriptures.

The pursuit of high social values furnishes the incentives of these new loyalties. In the one instance it is the realization of the classless society and the abundant life for all workers. Its great aim is to elevate the life of the masses and open to them the privileges which in the past have belonged only to the few. In the other case the end is to exalt the state, to restore its self-respect among great powers, to make it impregnable against its enemies, and to realize greater material abundance and richer opportunity in life for all its citizens. The methods adopted may be those of the ruthless use of power and terrorism, but the motivation in the beginning was the earnest desire to realize certain social ideals usually quite worthy in themselves. In the end the very methods employed may prove to be the nemesis of the whole enterprise, bringing about the defeat of movements which were rich with promise in their initial stages. But until the day of nemesis the outward successes of these new loyalties will put Christianity on its mettle to justify and maintain itself.

Mention should also be made of the elaborate use of ritual in these pseudo-religions as a means of awakening the imaginations and of enlisting the loyalties of the people. Ceremony and pageantry loom large in the program. Solemn services of consecration are also held which are so exalted in character that the change of only a few words would make them suitable for any great occasion of Christian enlistment. What has happened, of course, is that the most effective and best instruments of religion have been adapted to the uses of the new cult.

A high degree of personal discipline is also achieved through the demands made by these new crusades upon the lives of individual followers. In large measure this is a compulsory and regimented discipline, but it is perfectly evident that it is accepted willingly by the youth of the nations involved. They have heard the call to self-sacrifice in behalf of the greater glories of the state or the better life of the masses and have responded enthusiastically.

Another evidence that these new loyalties are virtually religions in the lives of their followers is the fact that through these means they are realizing membership in a great fellowship and are achieving a sense of community. They lose consciousness of themselves and of the futility of self-centered existence through belonging to a dynamic enterprise that gives meaning to their individual lives. In accord with a perfectly good Christian principle they are finding life by losing it, while in Christian lands throngs of young people are losing life in their very great determination to find it. Has Christianity sufficient inherent strength to meet the new challenge of the modern pseudo-religions?

THE FUTURE OF RELIGIOUS THOUGHT

The taking up of the challenge issued by so formidable a foe will be sure to have its effects upon the future emphases and practices of the Christian religion. We shall consider first of all some of the probable effects upon Christian thought and afterwards the consequences in Christian strategy.

In the generations preceding ours the most critical problem for religious thought was that of finding its proper relationship to a rapidly developing science with its very effective method for extending the range of human knowledge. By calling in question many of the accepted presuppositions of thought with which religious faith seemed to be tied, science appeared to be the enemy of religion. As we have already suggested there will continue to be tensions between new truth and the old formulations of the faith. But it has been found possible to reformulate the essentials of the faith in terms acceptable to new knowledge and religious insight may be enriched in the process. It has been necessary to define the proper functions of these two basic interests; but with the clarification of those functions it is evident that both religion and science have essential parts to play in the drama of life, and their representatives ought to work together, religion supplying the valid goals and science furnishing the most effective methods of implementing these goals. The warfare between science and religion is over, even though many people are not yet aware of that fact. The fact that scientists in the field of nuclear physics have taken the initiative in arranging conferences with religious leaders to lay upon the latter the awful responsibility which they face in providing the moral conditions

under which it is safe to make use of the newly released atomic energies, is evidence that a new day of understanding and reconciliation
between science and religion is at hand. Scientists are not moved by
fear of atomic energy, for they know how to control that; but, as Roger
Shinn points out, they are very much afraid of *other men* when "armed
with a new and dreadful power."[1] They recognize that the building of
the requisite character and moral controls is not a task for science, but
for religion.

Another movement already evident in Christian thought which will
be an important factor in determining its future character is a new
Realism. By realism in its present usage is meant the determination not
to gloss over any hard or disagreeable facts in life that appear to be
stumbling-blocks to religion, but to face them squarely and make religious thought begin with them as it constructs its house of faith. The
religion of the future must be more than wishful thinking. The first
test of its adequacy will be its ability to deal with the unpromising facts
of human existence. Walter M. Horton of the Oberlin Graduate School
of Theology is a good representative of this realistic trend in Christian
thought and he has written his conception of realism from which we
quote in part:

The word "realism" suggests to me, above all, a resolute determination
to face all the facts of life candidly, beginning preferably with the most stubborn, perplexing and disheartening ones, so that any lingering romantic
illusions may be dispelled at the start; and then *through* these stubborn facts
and not *in spite* of them, to pierce as deep as one may into the solid structure of reality, until one finds whatever ground of courage, hope, and faith
is *actually* there, independent of human preferences and desires. . . . It will
begin by looking out at the external world, not inward at the realm of
mind. It is prepared to accept a God who is a "consuming fire" and a terrible Judge, as well as a loving Father, and it is willing to recognize chaotic,
tragic, uncontrollable, and even devilish factors in reality, if candid observation leads to such conclusion.

A third tendency already apparent, the full force of which is yet to
be felt, is the determination to make religion truly God-centered. In
the liberalism of recent decades the desires and ideals of men have occu-

[1] *Beyond This Darkness,* p. 58.

pied the center of the stage while God stood on the periphery as the servant of human wishes. The trouble with this type of liberalism was not that it made personal values supreme, for Jesus did that, but that it made men largely self-sufficient and tended to render God unnecessary except as a convenient ally of human wishes. Humanism went even further and banished God altogether as unnecessary to the achievement of the good life for man in the world, if indeed not an obstacle to highest human development by robbing man of his self-reliance and encouraging him to pin his faith to an illusion. But God is coming back to his rightful place in religion, and his will is again being offered as the one possible program for a world that would avoid disaster and realize its highest values.

The swing back to God as dominant is not apt to be so extreme in America as it has been in Europe under the influence of the Barthian movement in theology. A condition of dire despair there has led religious thinkers to forsake completely all reliance upon human effort and to find deliverance in God alone. God has been made so transcendent that his immanent presence in the life of nature and of men has been denied altogether. A complete qualitative difference separates the human order from the divine realm and nothing man can do can bridge the gap. God is the "wholly other." Only God in ways that are above human understanding can break through with saving grace to man. Man can do nothing to help himself or by directing the course of history produce a new and better culture. Man's highest knowledge is only ignorance. He is completely lost until such a time as he realizes his utter hopelessness; and when his self-confidence is shattered, then God speaks a positive word in a lightning-like flash of revelation. In that revelation is man's salvation.

A religion which reduces man to nothingness and leaves God out of this world will probably prove as inadequate as a religion which exalted man to the supreme heights and banished God from heaven. In the light of recent tragic years in human experience religion has had to rethink its conception of man, however, and to reassert the long-established insight that liberalism tried to abandon, that man is a sinner by nature. He finds it easier to compromise with evil than to adhere strictly to ideals of righteousness. He loves himself more than his neighbor, and is more concerned with fulfilling his personal desires than with doing God's will. It would appear to be a part of the divine purpose that man shall grow in moral and spiritual stature through a process of overcoming resistance both within his own nature and in his environment. Man will ever be faced with that which must be overcome and conquered and for that reason utopia will never be realized on earth. This does not mean that moral progress is impossible, but declares that mankind will never bring to full realization the Christian ideal on earth. Every step in moral progress opens up new possibilities of both good and evil, and it is inevitable that man will at times fall prey to those evils. There will always be tragedy and crisis in human experience, but for the man of faith that will not be a cause for despair, but will be accepted as a recurring challenge to overcome, and to realize his larger self and a better world in the process.

Man is a sinner, but redemption is open to him as a real possibility. By meeting the requirements of redemption he can triumph over sin and live victoriously in the midst of an evil world as a child of God. This he will achieve not through his own meager strength, but through a dynamic fellowship with God. While a realistic view of man will recognize him to be a sinner, it will never lose sight of the tremendous potentialities which inhere in human nature when that nature becomes reconciled to God and fulfills the essential conditions of a vital fellowship with the source of creative power and purpose in the universe. The religion of the future promises to be realistic about man's present condition, but optimistic about his future possibilities in relation to God.

The ground of human hope will not rest in man himself, but in God. God's will, however, is not something to be trifled with. He is not to be swayed from his purpose, which makes totalitarian demands upon the loyalties of men. Christianity will confront the new totalitarianisms of the present world with a revival of the old totalitarianism of God's purpose for life. To the divine purpose men will be challenged anew to give full and undivided allegiance of both the mind and heart, to make it the supreme object of their loyalties. Only by presenting a loyalty in which inheres higher and more universal values than that of the antagonists, and by pursuing these by better and surer methods, can Christianity hope to meet the challenge of new ideologies which would supplant it. If God is, as Christian faith asserts, then the outcome of the present issue will be in his favor, and that particular system will triumph in the end which most nearly expresses his will. If Christianity is to win that triumph it will have to become again a God-centered religion, whose chief concern will be to know and to do his will.

Again in the realm of religious thought it would appear that in the future there will be a further development of rather than a lessening emphasis on the social applications of the gospel. This has been discussed at length in the preceding chapter so that little more need be said concerning it here. But this is one thing that needs must happen if Christianity is to contend successfully against its present opponents. E. S. Brightman in speaking of the successes of Communism declared, "In ninety years this movement with all its errors and crimes, seems to have shown more organized practical social concern for the poor, to whom the gospel is preached, than has the Christian Church."[2] If by effecting changes in the social order these political philosophies can in some measure fulfill the promises of the gospel, the church will have a hard time justifying itself in a hands-off policy. God's kingdom is to come on earth according to Jesus, and that means in social arrangements as well as in individual hearts.

THE FUTURE OF RELIGIOUS PRACTICE

As Christianity confronts vigorous opponents that are able to challenge people with programs of life that are very definite both with respect to goals and to means, it is being forced to re-examine its own position both with respect to its goals and the methods of their attainment. This is driving its devoted adherents back to a new consideration of the original sources and of the formative forces of its life. This means a renewed interest in the Bible. The old Bibliolatry is gone from intelligent circles never to return, but the Bible remains the one great sourcebook of the Christian religion. Those who wish to know its true genius cannot afford to neglect this book and those who would devote themselves to its tenets cannot neglect so important a resource. The Christ of the Christian religion is the Christ of the Bible and if he is to be presented to the world as a better leader and a truer saviour than contemporary dictators the attention of men will have to be turned again to the Bible, if they are to know what manner of person he is and for

[2] *The Future of Christianity,* p. 131. Abingdon-Cokesbury Press, 1937.

what he stands in the world. It may be difficult to describe in detail just what the future attitude toward the Bible will be and exactly how it will be used, but if Christianity survives and enters a new era of influence and power, a revival of interest in the Bible is bound to occur.

If we are correct in the judgment that the religion of the future will be more God-centered than recent liberal religion, then two other things are bound to follow as consequences, the recovery of private prayer and of corporate worship. If these are primary means of ascertaining God's will for contemporary life and of adjusting individual lives to the divine program, their practice can be neglected only at the peril of failure of the program. A higher conception of prayer as a form of co-operation with God, rather than as a means of getting things from an indulgent deity, will be an important factor in the restoration of prayer as an important means of religious discipline and personal reorientation.

One of the outstanding achievements of the new political and social programs that challenge Christianity has been the discipline of life among the young people. The contrast in this respect between the young people in the democratic nations and those of the totalitarian states is marked. The prevailing temper of a few years ago to exercise no restraints on one's impulses but to give free expression to one's personal desires as the way to fullness of life has been fairly well played out, for the ultimate result of such a mode of life was found to be boredom and futility. With respect to life lived on this basis Koheleth was right when long ago he proclaimed, "vanity of vanities, all is vanity and a striving after wind." If in democratic countries the younger generation is to be saved from the spirit of futility they must be challenged to a great crusade in which they may lose themselves and for which they will gladly undertake the discipline of life for the sake of their greatest effectiveness in forwarding the ideals of the crusade. "Without some system of morals to discipline his passions," says C. E. M. Joad, "some guiding principle in obedience to which to conserve his energies, some channel of endeavour along which to canalize his efforts, a man's activities tend to become diffused, and his life purposeless. He achieves nothing, and grows tired and discouraged through lack of achievement."[3] In another connection the same author says, "Morals properly

[3] *The Present and Future of Religion*, p. 113. Macmillan, 1930.

regarded are rules of spiritual hygiene, to be cultivated in the interests of intenser living."[4]

Throughout this work we have maintained that the essence of religious experience is to be captured by an ideal to which you devote yourself thoroughly. The new ideologies are doing that for the youth of their lands. Christianity in its creative periods has done that for youth of other generations and will accomplish it anew for the youth of this generation once they are given a vision of its full implications for the life of the world. The Kingdom of God as presented by Jesus Christ presents a nobler ideal for the world and a better method of attaining it than any of the popular philosophies of today whether they be communistic or fascistic in their tendencies. As youth are captured anew by that ideal the result will be a revival of moral discipline in living willingly accepted even as Jesus said, "For their sakes, I sanctify myself."

If Christianity is to be effective again as a redeeming force in the world another necessity which must be faced is the healing of the many divisions in the church. The number of competing sects within the body of Christ is a veritable scandal in view of the unity of the forces which oppose the Christian religion. If the issues on which they originally divided were meaningful to the people of today there might be some justification for this condition, but those issues are all washed out and young people particularly are bewildered as they seek to find meaning in the fact that although they think and believe very much alike they are drawn apart into many different groups in the exercise of their faith. The conservatism of religious people here asserts itself and in their earnest desire to safeguard all that is sacred they are really harming the great cause which they would serve. The problems of union are difficult on the practical grounds of differences in organization and polity, and because of vested interests both in property and in positions that might be abolished if union occurred. But the pressure of the opposition is forcing the church to come together. The trend toward union has become a powerful force and is bound to grow in power and bring together many churches in the years of the immediate future. Complete uniformity is, of course, not to be desired, but there seems little danger

[4] *Ibid.*, p. 306.

of going to that extreme. For the present the movement toward mergers and federation should receive every encouragement.

CHRISTIANITY AND OTHER RELIGIONS

The subject of church union suggests another problem, namely, the future relationship between the great religions of the world. Will one religion come to predominate and claim the entire earth? Not many years ago the watchword of the Student Volunteer Movement was "The Evangelization of the World in This Generation." That was a noble but impossible objective. As the past generation found it impossible, so it is improbable that any generation of Christians will succeed in converting the entire world to the existing type of Christianity. It is hardly likely that this would be altogether for the best, unless it be conceded that the other religions have no values which are not fully realized in Christianity. It is also unlikely that a new religion will be created on an eclectic basis by taking the best features of all the religions and combining them in a new synthesis. Religions are not manufactured, they grow, and you cannot dismember them and reassemble them as you can machines. But it is probable with the cross-fertilization of cultures that religions will be stimulated by one another and contribute to each other's life and development. The result of such a process will be that the great religions will come more and more to resemble each other and will not be marked by so great divergences in belief and practice.

Mahatma Gandhi of India was a living representative of this new tolerance among religions. He was a Hindu and proudly loyal to Hinduism. But his religious life was profoundly affected by his studies in other religions and by his contacts with members of other faiths. He freely acknowledged a great debt to the Sermon on the Mount, and certain Christian hymns are among his favorites. He also found real values in Islam and Buddhism. These he freely appropriated and made a part of his Hinduism. He claimed, of course, that these values were already inherently present in Hinduism but that it required these contacts with other religions in which they received greater emphasis to make him aware of them and of their importance. The result was that he lived a life so admirable both from the standpoint of inner piety and outward expression that many a devout Christian, who was no more willing to become a Hindu than Gandhi was a Christian, was willing to extend to him the hand of fellowship as a Christian brother, and Gandhi, on his part, accepted it and as a Hindu returned the compliment. In his life we see a symbol of things to come in the relations of the great religions to each other; they will share their treasures with each other, become more tolerant without lessened devotion, and grow more alike. The late E. S. Brightman in his work *The Future of Christianity* confirms this judgment:

> The Christian Church will come to recognize in Buddhism and Hinduism, Confucianism and Mohammedanism, other roads to God. The Christian will treat representatives of these religions as brothers, not as heathen enemies of the faith. If Christians have a higher truth than these other religions, as their faith leads them to believe, that superiority cannot be shown by a spirit of partisanship or arrogance. Mohammedans can teach Christians lessons in tolerance, for they never pronounce the name of Jesus without saying, "Blessed be his name." Buddhists can teach Christians lessons in spiritual calm and conquest of desire. Hindus can teach Christians mystical fellowship with the Divine. Confucianists can teach social responsibility. A relation of friendly and mutual interchange of spiritual values of this sort might go far toward bringing the whole world nearer to God.[5]

THE GOLDEN AGE

In the early days of human civilization religion exercised an absolute sovereignty over all human interests and enterprises and there was no differentiation of religious and secular concerns. Religion was an integral part of every human activity. It made a ritual of planting seed and of gathering the harvest, of engaging in battle or refraining from battle, of engaging in a hunt, of building a house or painting a decoration, of the birth of children and disposition of the dead. Nothing was omitted from its direct control. Only gradually were various interests differentiated from religion. According to the statement of Rabbi Abba Hillel Silver:

> The first architecture of mankind was religious architecture—the temple. The first poetry of mankind was religious poetry—the hymn. The first drama of mankind was religious drama—festival pageantry and ritual. The first science of mankind was religious science—magic, astrology and priestly

[5] P. 80.

therapeutics. All government was originally theocratic. The ruler was either himself the high priest or was ruled by the high priest. All law was religious law. All social custom was religious custom. There was no separation between sacred and profane. Religion enswathed the whole of life of man as with an element.[6]

Not easily did these various interests succeed in escaping religious domination and become independent secular pursuits. By degrees government broke from ecclesiastical control. The sciences followed the lead of government, and much of the bitterness in the struggle between science and religion grew out of the determination of science to assert its independence from a church reluctant to grant it. The arts which for long were wholly dedicated to religion followed suit in asserting their right to independent existence. Education likewise became principally a secular enterprise under the control of the state rather than the church. One by one religion's children have grown up and asserted their independence of parental control. They have gone their own ways and developed their own characters often with little thought of the parent's welfare. It is well that they have asserted their independence, cultivated their own essential characters, and learned to stand on their own feet, for they are all the stronger and abler for it.

The period of adolescent revolt, however, seems to be about over and the mature and independent children may again be expected to place themselves at the service of Mother Faith. Without sacrifice of independence they will voluntarily put their developed abilities at the service of religion in co-operative effort to realize the divine purpose in the world of men. In that day of high co-operation between religion and the arts and sciences, government and education, religion will come into her own. The golden age for religion is not in the past but in the future.

One would like to stop with that last affirmation, as an earlier version of this work did. The present outlook in the world makes a further word necessary. Whether the glorious day of religious dominion is to be realized soon or late, no one knows, but the immediate prospects appear to be anything but favorable. It may well be that humanity will have to undergo more fearfully destructive judgments than have yet been suffered, before men will learn the things that belong to their

[6] *Religion in a Changing World*, p. 29 f.

peace and welfare, and voluntarily choose to live by God's will and purpose for life. It may be that the immediate future will involve mankind in further setbacks rather than progress toward a better world; but God's purposes will not be defeated forever. For the individual, however, irrespective of the character of his generation, the golden age of religion is always the living present, if he accepts for himself the insights of high religion and fulfills the conditions necessary to the appropriation of the spiritual resources of life. Perhaps, if enough people dedicate themselves to the way of vital intelligent religion, the awful specters that now loom before the world may be banished, and a better, although not a utopian, world come into being more rapidly than at present we dare to hope.

Bibliography

The books and references in this bibliography have been selected in the light of the needs, interests and abilities of young people in general rather than those of advanced students.

Books of General Interest

Brown, William Adams. *Beliefs That Matter*. Scribner's, 1930.

Ferm, Vergilius. *First Chapters in Religious Philosophy*. Round Table, 1937.

Finegan, Jack. *Beginnings in Theology*. Association Press, 1956.

Gray, Henry David. *A Theology for Christian Youth*. Abingdon, 1941.

Harkness, Georgia. *Conflicts in Religious Thought*. Harper, 1949.

———. *Understanding the Christian Faith*. Abingdon, 1947.

Harner, Nevin C. *I Believe*. Christian Education, 1950.

Harrington, John B. *Essentials in Christian Faith*. Harper, 1958.

Hart, Hornell. *Skeptic's Guest*. Macmillan, 1938.

Houf, Horace T. *What Religion Is and Does*. Harper, 1945.

King, Winston L. *Introduction to Religion*. Harper, 1954.

McKee, Elmore M. *What Use is Religion?* Scribner's, 1939.

McKown, Edgar M., and Scherzer, Carl J. *Understanding Christianity*. Ronald, 1949.

Munk, Arthur W. *Perplexing Problems in Religion*. Bethany, 1954.

O'Brien, John A. *Truths Men Live By*. Macmillan, 1948.

Palmer, Albert W. *The Light of Faith*. Macmillan, 1945.

Rall, Harris F. *Christianity*. Scribner's, 1940.

Silver, Abba H. *Religion in a Changing World*. Harper, 1931.

Spurrier, William A. *Guide to the Christian Faith*. Scribner's, 1953.

Wright, W. K. *A Student's Philosophy of Religion*. Macmillan, 1922.

I. Motives for Being Religious

Harkness, Georgia. *Religious Living*. Association Press, 1940.
Soares, T. G. *Religious Education*. Chaps. II, IV. University of Chicago, 1928.

II. Nature and Function of Religion

Bennett, John C. *Christianity and Our World*. Association Press, 1936.
Van Dusen, Henry P. *Reality and Religion*. Association Press, 1938.

III. Religion and Science

Mather, Kirtley F. *Science in Search of God*. Holt, 1928.
Thomson, J. Arthur. *Science and Religion*. Scribner's, 1925.
———. *Science and Religion*. A symposium. Scribner's, 1931.

IV. Living by Faith

Fosdick, H. E. *The Meaning of Faith*. Association Press, 1922.
Vlastos, Gregory. *Christian Faith and Democracy*. Association Press, 1936.

V. Is the Bible the Word of God?

Anderson, B. W. *Rediscovering the Bible*. Association Press, 1951.
Bowie, Walter R. *The Bible*. Association Press, 1939.
Denbeaux, Fred J. *Understanding the Bible*. Westminster, 1958.
Fosdick, H. E. *The Modern Use of the Bible*. Macmillan, 1924.
Machen, J. G. *Christian Faith in the Modern World*. Macmillan, 1936.

VI. How Shall We Think of God?

Gilkey, J. G. *The Certainty of God*. Macmillan, 1928.
Horton, Walter M. *God*. Association Press, 1937.
Jenkins, Daniel. *Believing in God*. Westminster, 1956.
Langford, Norman. *Barriers to Belief*. Westminster, 1958.

VII. Jesus Christ, the Son and Saviour

Bowie, Walter R. *The Master*. Scribner's, 1930.
Coffin, Henry S. *What Men Are Thinking*. Abingdon, 1933.
Johnson, Robert. *The Meaning of Christ*. Westminster, 1958.
Lyman, Mary Ely. *Jesus*. Association Press, 1937.

VIII. The New Realism about Sin

Bennett, John C. *Social Salvation*. Chap. I. Scribner's, 1935.
Horton, Walter M. *Realistic Theology*. Chap. II. Harper, 1934.

IX. Right and Wrong

Kee, Howard C. *Making Ethical Decisions*. Westminster, 1957.
King, William P. *Right and Wrong*. Abingdon, 1938.
Titus, Harold H. *What is a Mature Morality?* Macmillan, 1943.
Trueblood, Elton. *Foundations of Reconstruction*. Harper, 1946.

X. Prayer

Brown, William Adams. *The Life of Prayer in a World of Science*. Harper, 1927.
Coburn, John B. *Prayer and Personal Religion*. Westminster, 1957.
Fosdick, H. E. *The Meaning of Prayer*. Association Press, 1915.
Steere, Douglas V. *Prayer and Worship*. Association Press, 1938.
Wieman, H. N. *Methods of Private Religious Living*. Macmillan, 1931.

XI. The Case for Immortality

Baillie, John. *And the Life Everlasting*. Scribner's, 1933.
Fosdick, H. E. *The Assurance of Immortality*. Association Press, 1919.
Shinn, Roger L. *Life, Death, and Destiny*. Westminster, 1957.

XII. Why the Church?

Brown, Robert M. *The Significance of the Church*. Westminster, 1956.
Latourette, Kenneth S. *Toward a World Christian Fellowship*. Association Press, 1938.
Stewart, George. *The Church*. Association Press, 1938.

XIII. Religion and Social Change

Bennett, John C. *Social Salvation*. Scribner's, 1935.
———. *Christianity and Our World*. Association Press, 1936.
Jones, E. Stanley. *Christ's Alternative to Communism*. Abingdon, 1935.
Miller, William L. *The Protestant and Politics*. Westminster, 1958.
Tittle, Ernest E. *Christians in an Unchristian Society*. Association Press, 1940.
Vlastos, Gregory. *Christianity and Democracy*. Association Press, 1938.

XIV. The Future of Religion

Brightman, E. S. *The Future of Christianity*. Abingdon, 1937.
Joad, C. E. M. *The Present and Future of Religion*. Macmillan, 1930.

Index

Set in Linotype Granjon
Format by James T. Parker
Manufactured by The Haddon Craftsmen, Inc.
Published by HARPER & BROTHERS, *New York*